HOLT

Lifetime Health

Life Skills Workbook

D1557964

HOLT, RINEHART AND WINSTON

A Harcourt Education Company

Orlando • **Austin** • New York • San Diego • Toronto • London

TO THE STUDENT

Life skills are skills that you can use throughout your life to build and maintain a healthy lifestyle. The *Life Skills* workbook is designed to help you apply and practice the life skills. You will find various activity worksheets that review and reinforce the 10 Life Skills:

- Assessing Your Health
- Communicating Effectively
- Practicing Wellness
- Coping
- Being a Wise Consumer

- Evaluating Media Messages
- Using Community Resources
- Making GREAT Decisions
- Using Refusal Skills
- Setting Goals

Copyright © by Holt, Rinehart and Winston

All rights reserved. No part of this publication may be reproduced or transmitted in any form or by any means, electronic or mechanical, including photocopy, recording, or any information storage and retrieval system, without permission in writing from the publisher.

Teachers using LIFETIME HEALTH may photocopy complete pages in sufficient quantities for classroom use only and not for resale.

Lifetime Health—High School (Main Text and Supplemental)

Cover photo: Scott Van Osdol

Printed in the United States of America

ISBN 0-03-068117-0

1 2 3 4 5 6   024   07 06 05 04 03

Contents

Property of
Raugust Library
6070 College Lane
Jamestown, ND 58405

Copyright © by Holt, Rinehart and Winston. All rights reserved.

Preventing Violence and Abuse

Physical Fitness for Life

Nutrition for Life

Weight Management and Eating Behaviors

Copyright © by Holt, Rinehart and Winston. All rights reserved.

Understanding Drugs and Medicines

Alcohol

Tobacco

Illegal Drugs

Copyright © by Holt, Rinehart and Winston. All rights reserved.

Preventing Infectious Diseases

Life Skills Worksheet: Practicing Wellness

Life Skills Worksheet: Setting Goals

Life Skills Worksheet: Using Community Resources

Lifestyle Diseases

Life Skills Worksheet: Assessing Your Health

Life Skills Worksheet: Practicing Wellness

Life Skills Worksheet: Communicating Effectively

Life Skills Worksheet: Using Community Resources

Other Diseases and Disabilities

Life Skills Worksheet: Assessing Your Health

Life Skills Worksheet: Using Community Resources

Life Skills Worksheet: Evaluating Media Messages

Adolescence and Adulthood

Life Skills Worksheet: Setting Goals

Life Skills Worksheet: Coping

Marriage, Parenthood, and Families

Life Skills Worksheet: Using Community Resources

Life Skills Worksheet: Making GREAT Decisions

Life Skills Worksheet: Coping

Copyright © by Holt, Rinehart and Winston. All rights reserved.

Reproduction, Pregnancy, and Development

Building Responsible Relationships

Risks of Adolescent Sexual Activity

HIV and AIDS

Express Lessons

Copyright © by Holt, Rinehart and Winston. All rights reserved.

What You Need to Know About . . .

First Aid and Safety

Quick Review

Copyright © by Holt, Rinehart and Winston. All rights reserved.

Name _____ Class _____ Date _____

Life Skills

Setting Goals
STAYING HEALTHY
PART I
Your health is influenced by many factors, some of which you can control. Study the two lists below. Then for each question write the letter of the correct answer in the blank.

Leading Causes of Death Listed on Death Certificates	Leading Root Causes of Death
heart disease	diet and activity
cancer	toxic materials
stroke	high blood pressure
lung disease	tobacco
pneumonia and influenza	bacteria and viruses

_____ 1. The leading root causes of death are
   a. risk factors for disease or injury.
   b. all uncontrollable.
   c. unrelated to health.
   d. all controllable.

_____ 2. Which of the following root causes of death are controllable risk factors for heart disease?
   a. diet and activity
   b. bacteria and viruses
   c. tobacco and diet
   d. toxic materials

_____ 3. What lifestyle changes could you make to reduce the controllable risk factors for heart disease?
   a. avoid exercise
   b. exercise and eat sensibly
   c. research your medical history
   d. eat foods high in saturated fat

PART II

4. Use what you have learned about controllable risk factors to write three health goals.

_____

_____

_____

_____

Copyright © by Holt, Rinehart and Winston. All rights reserved.

Skills Worksheet)

Life Skills

Assessing Your Health
MANAGING YOUR FEELINGS
PART I

A person's reaction to stressful situations can affect his or her emotional health and physical health. Identifying feelings and learning positive ways to manage them can help a person stay healthy. Answer the questions in the space provided.

1. List three situations that can cause a person to become angry.

_____

_____

_____

2. List three situations that can cause a person to feel anxious.

_____

_____

_____

3. List three situations that can make a person feel frustrated.

_____

_____

_____

PART II

4. Stressful feelings can be managed in ways that minimize their impact on your emotional and physical health. Imagine that you are confronted with one of the situations you listed above.

Circle the reactions below that you think would promote good emotional health. Put an "X" through reactions that would increase the risk to your health.

Yell at someone.	Hit someone.	Ask an adult for help.
Cry.	Drink alcohol.	Blame someone for
Smoke a cigarette.	Plot revenge.	your feelings.
Take a nap.	Slam a door.	Go for a drive.
Punch a pillow.	Write a list of solutions	Identify your feelings
Discuss your feelings	to the problem.	and their source.
with a family member.	Listen to music.	Practice deep breathing.

Copyright © by Holt, Rinehart and Winston. All rights reserved.

Name _____ Class _____ Date _____

Life Skills

Communicating Effectively
BE AN ADVOCATE!

Identify a health issue that affects students in your school. Then follow the steps below to create a public service announcement that addresses the problem.

1. What is the health issue you want to speak about to your audience?

_____

_____

_____

_____

2. Who makes up your audience? What might be the best way of presenting information to your audience to make the message more appealing to this group?

_____

_____

_____

_____

3. Research! Use library resources to make sure you have the most up-to-date and valid information about your issue. Make notes in the space provided. Use a separate sheet of paper if you need more space.

_____

_____

_____

_____

4. Be an advocate! Write a brief public service announcement that addresses the problem and your proposed solutions.

_____

_____

_____

_____

Copyright © by Holt, Rinehart and Winston. All rights reserved.

Skills Worksheet

Life Skills

Practicing Wellness
HEALTHY BEHAVIORS

Practicing healthy behaviors every day can help you have good, life-long health. Think about such behaviors as you answer the questions below.

1. What are some healthy behaviors that apply to your life right now?

_____

_____

_____

2. List two healthy behaviors that you think will apply to your life when you have reached adulthood.

_____

_____

_____

3. List two healthy behaviors that apply to your life now and will also apply to your life in later years. What advantage is there to practicing these behaviors now?

_____

_____

_____

4. Which of the behaviors that you listed in the previous question could you start practicing right now?

_____

_____

5. Choose one healthy behavior and make a list of actions that you can take now to practice it.

_____

_____

_____

_____

Copyright © by Holt, Rinehart and Winston. All rights reserved.

Name _____ Class _____ Date _____

Life Skills

Making GREAT Decisions
INVOLVING OTHERS

In your life, you will face some decisions that are so serious that you will want to consult others. These are decisions that will affect your life and your health. In the following questions, you are asked to apply the GREAT Decisions model to a decision you have made with the help of others.

Give thought to the problem: In what decision did you need to involve a team, your parents, a teacher, or your friends? Who was the best person to work with on this problem?

_____

_____

_____

Review your choices: Many times the choices are not only pro and con. Were there multiple ways to solve this problem? If so, what were they?

_____

_____

_____

Evaluate the consequences of each choice: Were any of these choices unpopular? If so, which ones? Would these choices have affected others? If so, how?

_____

_____

_____

Assess and choose the best choice: What were the things that entered into your decision? Did you need support in order to carry out this decision?

_____

_____

Think it over afterward: How did you feel about this decision after you carried it out? If you had to face this decision again, what, if anything, would you do differently?

_____

_____

Copyright © by Holt, Rinehart and Winston. All rights reserved.

Life Skills

Using Refusal Skills
RESISTING PRESSURE

Sometimes it is important to make a good decision quickly. Read the passage below and answer the following questions.

Pete is at a party at his friend Rhonda's house. He is having a good time until he looks at his watch and realizes that he should have called his parents 5 minutes ago. They said that he could come to this party if he promised to call them at 10 p.m. Pete goes to use the phone, but Rhonda is using it and seems to be ignoring him. His friend Jack offers to give him a ride on his motorcycle to the nearest phone booth, which is a few blocks away. Jack appears to be a safe driver, but he does not have a helmet for Pete to wear. Pete gets the feeling that declining Jack's offer will make him seem silly to his friends. After all, it's only a couple of blocks.

1. What options does Pete have? List the possible positive and negative consequences of each one.

   _____

   _____

2. What does Pete decide to do? Finish the story, showing the best possible decision and its consequences. Do you think Pete is happy with his decision? Why or why not?

   _____

   _____

   _____

   _____

3. Now finish the story again, showing the worst possible decision and its consequences. Do you think Pete is happy with his decision? Why or why not?

   _____

   _____

   _____

4. Which refusal skills did you include in Pete's options? Did he use one of them? If so, which one?

   _____

   _____

Copyright © by Holt, Rinehart and Winston. All rights reserved.

Skills Worksheet

Life Skills

Setting Goals

SHORT-TERM GOALS

A short-term goal is one that can be achieved quickly, in days or weeks. The satisfaction of reaching a short-term goal can encourage you to work on long-term goals. Think about some of the factors involved in developing an action plan for a short-term goal.

1. Name a short-term goal that is related to your health. Why is reaching this goal important to you?

   _____

   _____

2. What influences will help you and what influences will hinder you as you work toward your goal?

   _____

   _____

3. How will you track your progress? Is it necessary to have milestones for a short-term goal? Explain.

   _____

   _____

4. How are you planning to reward yourself when you reach your goal? How will the reward encourage you to continue the positive behaviors that led you to achieve this goal?

   _____

   _____

5. When you reach your goal, how do you plan to evaluate the entire process? Will achieving this goal influence how you set your future goals?

   _____

   _____

   _____

   _____

Copyright © by Holt, Rinehart and Winston. All rights reserved.

Skills Worksheet

Life Skills

Practicing Wellness
CHOOSING SUPPORTIVE RELATIONSHIPS

As important as it is to make your own decisions about your worth, your self-esteem is sometimes influenced by others around you. For each of the following situations, what advice would you give about preserving self-esteem?

1. Samantha had sexual intercourse with her boyfriend because he said he would dump her if she did not. Before this happened, Samantha hadn't thought seriously about her moral beliefs regarding premarital sex. Now she regrets having given in to the pressure. She's worried that he will expect to have sexual intercourse again.

_____

_____

_____

_____

2. Raol and Angel have both asked Sue to a dance. Angel is handsome and popular, but he is always making fun of others. He often teases and embarrasses her. Raol is neither popular nor unpopular. He is sensitive to others' feelings, though, and treats Sue with respect.

_____

_____

_____

_____

3. Francine needs someone to evaluate her term paper before she turns it in. She loves showing her work to Jerry because he always tells her it is excellent. Showing it to Arsenio is sometimes difficult, because he points out flaws. He always suggests ways to improve the paper.

_____

_____

_____

_____

Copyright © by Holt, Rinehart and Winston. All rights reserved.

Skills Worksheet

Life Skills

Communicating Effectively
EVALUATING COMMUNICATION SKILLS
Answer the questions in the spaces provided.

1. Emily is baby-sitting Bo, a two-year-old, when he starts crying. Emily gets down on the floor with him and asks what's wrong. After watching his gestures and listening to his sounds, Emily asks, "You lost your truck?" Bo nods. They find Bo's truck under the couch. What communication skills did Emily use?

_____

_____

_____

_____

2. Emily is talking about her day while her mom cooks dinner. As Emily is talking about the report she gave to her science class, her mom is distracted by something burning. When her attention is free again, she asks Emily to repeat what she just said. Emily feels hurt and leaves the room. What went wrong in this exchange? What could Emily and her mom do to improve their communication?

_____

_____

_____

_____

3. Conor calls Emily while she's doing homework. At first she gives him her full attention, but then her eyes drift back to the equation she was solving. When Conor suddenly stops talking, it takes Emily a moment to notice the silence. Conor accuses her of not listening to him. She apologizes and offers to call him later. What would have improved this exchange?

_____

_____

_____

_____

Copyright © by Holt, Rinehart and Winston. All rights reserved.

Skills Worksheet)
Life Skills

Assessing Your Health
USING MASLOW'S HIERARCHY OF NEEDS

When several problems overlap, it can be difficult to see any one problem clearly. Maslow's hierarchy of needs is a useful tool for identifying, untangling, and solving such problems. Read the paragraph below and answer the questions. For each question, identify the stage of needs that is at issue.

Chantal is doing homework after school. She feels tired, so she has some potato chips and a soft drink. Now she feels worse. She thinks that maybe she needs to exercise, but she isn't comfortable walking in her neighborhood by herself. Chantal goes back to her desk, but she is distracted by the memory of a disagreement she had with a friend at school today.

1. Was Chantal's snack nutritious? What could she have eaten instead to boost her energy? What else could she have done about her tiredness?

    Stage: _____

    _____

2. How could Chantal address the problem of feeling unsafe walking by herself?

    Stage: _____

    _____

3. What could Chantal do right now to resolve the conflict with her friend?

    Stage: _____

    _____

4. If Chantal dealt with her more immediate problems but still felt basically insecure, what could she do to work on her self-concept?

    Stage: _____

    _____

5. Once Chantal has addressed her more basic needs, she could think about her talents and dreams. What could she do to explore and develop her talents?

    Stage: _____

    _____

    _____

Copyright © by Holt, Rinehart and Winston. All rights reserved.

Name _____ Class _____ Date _____

Life Skills

Using Community Resources
HELP FOR MENTAL DISORDERS

At some point, you may wish to seek treatment for a mental disorder for yourself or someone you know. Use these activities to become familiar with the options for treatment in your community.

1. Ask a school counselor what counseling for mental disorders is available through your school or district. List the resources.

   _____

   _____

2. List the agencies in your community that provide counseling or medication for mental disorders. Research hospitals, counseling, support groups, mental health, psychologists, treatment centers, crisis intervention, and other groups or organizations. Use the HealthLinks Web site and library resources to find out what services these agencies provide.

   _____

   _____

3. Which of the agencies focus on a specific disorder?

   _____

   _____

4. Which agencies sponsor in-patient care facilities?

   _____

   _____

5. What services are available without charge or at a reduced rate?

   _____

   _____

6. Who qualifies for service?

   _____

   _____

   _____

Copyright © by Holt, Rinehart and Winston. All rights reserved.

Name _____ Class _____ Date _____

Life Skills

Practicing Self-Care
TURNING DISTRESS INTO EUSTRESS
Describe how the stress depicted in each situation below can be turned from distress into eustress.

1. Ricky has an important baseball game on Friday. He is very nervous about playing in the game because several family members and friends will be there watching him.

_____

_____

_____

2. Marcella has to give an oral presentation in her history class. She has never spoken in front of a group of people before. When she thinks about having to give her report, she feels nauseated.

_____

_____

_____

3. Eli's uncle is in the hospital because of a recent heart attack. Eli feels helpless and depressed and is worried that his uncle may not recover.

_____

_____

_____

4. Shana is afraid to ask her parents if she can go away for the weekend with her friend Abby and her family.

_____

_____

_____

_____

Copyright © by Holt, Rinehart and Winston. All rights reserved.

Skills Worksheet

Life Skills

Coping
GETTING PERSPECTIVE

If low resiliency is causing a person to feel stress, sometimes the best way to relieve the stress and build up self-esteem is to discuss stressful feelings with a friend. Using this worksheet, hold a mock resiliency-building session with a friend.

1. Complete the following sentences by pretending that you are a person experiencing the following stressors:

a. Sometimes I am afraid people won't like me because

_____

_____

b. Sometimes I am afraid people will reject me because

_____

_____

c. Sometimes I feel inadequate when (list situations and reasons)

_____

_____

2. Read your answers to 1a through 1c out loud to a friend. Talk with your friend about why the person feels the way he or she does. Then have your friend help you complete the following sentences to help remind the person of their assets:

a. People like me because

_____

_____

b. Some of my best traits are

_____

_____

c. When I'm feeling unsure of myself, I can

_____

_____

3. Repeat steps 1 and 2, trading places with your friend.

Copyright © by Holt, Rinehart and Winston. All rights reserved.

Life Skills

Coping
WORKING THROUGH THE STAGES OF GRIEF

Listed below are the five stages of grief. For each of these stages, list three activities that could help you express and work through the feelings associated with that stage.

Stage 1: denial _____

_____

_____

_____

Stage 2: anger _____

_____

_____

_____

Stage 3: bargaining _____

_____

_____

_____

Stage 4: depression _____

_____

_____

_____

Stage 5: acceptance _____

_____

_____

_____

_____

Copyright © by Holt, Rinehart and Winston. All rights reserved.

Name _____ Class _____ Date _____

Life Skills

Using Community Resources
FINDING HELP FOR SUICIDAL FEELINGS

Counseling services are available in your community to help people who are considering suicide. Research the availability of such resources in your community using library resources. Then use the following questions to evaluate the service you selected.

Name of service _____

Address _____ Phone number _____

1. How easy is it to contact this counseling service? What are their service hours?

   _____

   _____

   _____

   _____

2. Can concerned family and friends easily contact this service?

   _____

   _____

   _____

   _____

3. Can this service put a person in contact with professional help?

   _____

   _____

   _____

   _____

4. Is this service confidential?

   _____

   _____

   _____

Copyright © by Holt, Rinehart and Winston. All rights reserved.

Skills Worksheet

Life Skills

Communicating Effectively

A CONTINUUM OF VIOLENCE

PART I

One of the most important parts of staying safe is being able to recognize when a situation is becoming violent. Think about each of the following behaviors. Then, rank the behaviors from least to most violent, placing the letters of each behavior on the appropriate portion of the continuum.

a. teasing

b. pushing

c. slapping

d. name-calling

e. insulting

f. shouting

g. stabbing

h. eye-rolling

i. spreading rumors

j. putting a "kick me" sign on someone's back

k. pointing a gun at someone

l. threatening to beat someone up

m. pulling a chair out from under a classmate

n. making racist comments

←————————————————————————————→

Least Violent   **Moderately Violent**   **Most Violent**

PART II

1. What steps can you take to stay safe if you have identified a dangerous situation?

   _____

   _____

   _____

2. Imagine that you have followed all of the steps to avoid a dangerous confrontation, but still find yourself in a serious conflict. As you recall the tips for communicating effectively, you realize that empathy—putting yourself in the other person's shoes—is an important part of reaching a peaceful solution. Explain how empathy is the first step in preventing violence.

   _____

   _____

   _____

   _____

Copyright © by Holt, Rinehart and Winston. All rights reserved.

Name _____ Class _____ Date _____

Life Skills

Using Community Resources
HELP FOR ABUSIVE FAMILIES

Pick one of the resources in your community that helps members of abusive families. Choose a resource below or another resource you are interested in.

community health center
substance-abuse program
rape-crisis hotline
runaway hotline
emergency food pantry

department of family services
parents' support group
child-abuse hotline
center for battered women

1. Write the name of the community resource, its address, and phone number.

_____

_____

_____

2. Describe the type of service or services that you think the resource offers.

_____

_____

_____

_____

3. Research the community resource. Use the questions below to find out more about it. Add your own questions.

• What services does the agency offer?
• To whom are these services available and when?
• How much does it cost to use these services?
• What does a person have to do to get access to these services?
• What qualifications does the staff of the agency have?
• How is the agency funded?
• What should a person do in an emergency if he or she needs the kinds of services the agency offers?

4. Write a summary of your research on a separate sheet of paper. Post the summary on a classroom bulletin board.

Copyright © by Holt, Rinehart and Winston. All rights reserved.

Life Skills

Being a Wise Consumer
STAYING SAFE ONLINE

The Internet is a valuable tool that puts vast amounts of information at your fingertips. But it also has a darker side. The Internet can invite strangers into your home who may be sexual predators. Teenagers are frequent targets for sexual harassment and abuse.

Answer the following questions to learn how to deal with online sexual misconduct.

1. Why do you think people often do not consider online sexual harassment a real form of abuse?

_____

_____

_____

2. What qualities does the Internet have that make it particularly attractive to sexual predators?

_____

_____

_____

3. Adolescents are frequent targets of online predators, who know that teens are often reluctant to report online harassment to adults. What are some reasons teens might not want to talk about online abuse?

_____

_____

_____

_____

4. List ways you can avoid online sexual harassment.

_____

_____

_____

Copyright © by Holt, Rinehart and Winston. All rights reserved.

Skills Worksheet

Life Skills

Practicing Wellness
HEALTH-RELATED FITNESS ACTIVITIES

Classify each description below by giving it the letter or letters of the correct component or components.

_____ **1.** climbing a short flight of stairs

_____ **2.** walking one mile briskly

_____ **3.** cross-country skiing

_____ **4.** 15 minutes of stretching exercises

_____ **5.** lifting a heavy weight with few repetitions

_____ **6.** jogging a 5 km fun-run

_____ **7.** eating healthfully

_____ **8.** dancing for 30 minutes

_____ **9.** carrying a heavy shopping bag from a store to your home

_____ **10.** swimming 10 laps

_____ **11.** pushing a large piece of furniture to the other side of a room

_____ **12.** cycling to school every morning

_____ **13.** lifting weights with many repetitions

_____ **14.** jumping rope to warm up

_____ **15.** regular exercise in all areas

a. muscular strength

b. muscular endurance

c. cardiorespiratory endurance

d. flexibility

e. body composition

16. Which activities appeal most to you? Why, or why not, is it good to do several of these activities?

_____

_____

_____

_____

_____

Copyright © by Holt, Rinehart and Winston. All rights reserved.

Skills Worksheet

Life Skills

Setting Goals
IMPROVING YOUR FITNESS

1. Choose one component of your physical fitness that you would like to improve.

_____

2. What exercise would be a good indicator of your fitness in this area? (For example, the number of miles you could run would be an indicator of your cardiorespiratory endurance.)

_____

3. How could you measure your progress?

_____

4. What level of fitness are you currently able to achieve in this exercise?

_____

5. What level would you like to achieve?

_____

6. Outline below a six-week plan to achieve your goal. Identify how you will increase your cardiorespiratory endurance, muscular strength and endurance, and flexibility. Be specific about the kinds of exercises, the length of time you will spend exercising, and the number of times per week that you will do the exercises. For muscular development exercises, include the number of repetitions and your goals for increasing repetitions each week. Use additional paper if necessary.

_____

_____

_____

_____

_____

7. Check with your teacher to evaluate whether your goals are realistic. If they are not, explain how you will modify them.

_____

_____

Copyright © by Holt, Rinehart and Winston. All rights reserved.

Skills Worksheet

Life Skills

Making GREAT Decisions
RECOVERING FROM INJURIES

Ramon has been playing soccer for several years with a sports club, as well as playing on your school team. At a recent game, he sprained his ankle while running. He wants to play in the game next weekend, but his ankle still hurts. He wants to play because he knows that there will be talent scouts from colleges coming to watch the game, and he would like to get an athletic scholarship to college.

What advice would you give to this friend? Remember to use the decision-making steps.

Give thought to the problem.

Review your choices.

Evaluate the consequences of each choice.

Assess and choose the best choice.

Think it over afterward.

_____

_____

_____

_____

_____

_____

_____

_____

_____

_____

_____

_____

_____

_____

Copyright © by Holt, Rinehart and Winston. All rights reserved.

Skills Worksheet

Life Skills

Practicing Self-Care
KEEPING A SLEEP JOURNAL

1. Over the next week, fill in the following table. The first four items relate to the conditions of your sleep, and the last four refer to your experience the following day. Keep a journal describing any conditions that affected the quality of your sleep.

	Day 1	Day 2	Day 3	Day 4	Day 5	Day 6	Day 7
Did you eat within 3 hours of bedtime?							
Level of stress at bedtime (1–5, 1 = relaxed, 5 = most stress)							
Hours slept							
Number of awakenings							
Feeling rested upon rising (1–5, 1 = rested, 5 = very tired)							
Energy level (1–5, 1 = energetic, 5 = lack any energy)							
Mood (1–5, 1 = good mood, 5 = bad mood)							
Alertness (1–5, 1 = alert, 5 = not alert)							

2. Do you notice any patterns in your table or journal? If so, why might they exist?

_____

_____

_____

3. Based on your study, what changes could you make to sleep better?

_____

_____

_____

_____

_____

_____

Copyright © by Holt, Rinehart and Winston. All rights reserved.

Skills Worksheet
Life Skills

Being a Wise Consumer
EVALUATING SUGARS AND FATS IN FOODS

Refined sugars are simple carbohydrates that provide your body with quick energy, but few nutrients. They are added to food products as sweeteners. Refined sugars can be identified as sugar, brown sugar, cane sugar, and sucrose in the list of ingredients on food labels. If you eat a lot of foods with these added sugars, you may not eat enough foods that are rich in nutrients.

Different kinds of fats can also be listed in the ingredients on food labels. A diet high in saturated fats can increase the risk of heart disease and obesity. Foods made from animal products contain saturated fats. Coconut oil and palm oil are saturated plant oils that are added to some food products.

Visit a supermarket and find five different kinds of food products you eat or have eaten recently that have nutritional labels. List each food and the refined sugars (if any) it contains. Note if the food contains coconut oil or palm oil.

Food Product	Refined Sugar(s)	Saturated Fat(s)
1.	1.	1.
2.	2.	2.
3.	3.	3.
4.	4.	4.
5.	5.	5.

6. How can a diet high in sugars and saturated fats affect health?

_____

_____

_____

_____

_____

_____

Copyright © by Holt, Rinehart and Winston. All rights reserved.

Skills Worksheet

Life Skills

Assessing Your Health
DAILY CALCIUM NEEDS

The teen years are an important time for building strong bones and teeth, which contain 99 percent of the calcium in the body. Milk and other dairy products are the best sources of this mineral, but you can also get it from other foods.

Calcium is crucial! But how can you get enough of it? Use the table below to calculate your calcium intake, based on guidelines from the American Dietetic Association.

Type of Food	Portion Size	Milligrams of Calcium
Plain, fat-free yogurt	1 cup	450
Grilled cheese sandwich	1 sandwich	371
Milk (fat-free of low-fat)	1 cup	300
Cheese pizza	1 slice	111–147
Broccoli, cooked or fresh	1 cup	105
Bok choy, cooked or fresh	0.5 cup	80
Almonds, dry roasted	1 ounce	71
White bread	2 slices	70

1. The table above lists the calcium content for some common foods. The numbers are expressed in milligrams. Given that the recommended daily intake of calcium for teens is 1,300 milligrams, how would you choose from among the foods listed to get enough calcium for one day?

_____

_____

_____

People who don't like or can't eat certain calcium-rich foods can still get enough calcium by eating foods to which calcium has been added. A food's nutrition label lists calcium content in terms of Daily Values (DVs). The DV for a nutrient is the percentage of the recommended amount of the nutrient in a serving. DVs are calculated based on a 2000-Calorie diet.

2. Visit a supermarket and find two foods that have had calcium added to them. What percentage of the recommended daily value does each food contain?

_____

_____

Copyright © by Holt, Rinehart and Winston. All rights reserved.

Skills Worksheet

Life Skills

Practicing Wellness
CHOOSING NUTRITIOUS CEREALS

1. Read the labels on three instant breakfast cereals, including at least one whole-grain choice. Use the information about one serving to complete the table.

Name of Cereal, Main Ingredient	Grams of Carbohydrate, % of Daily Value	Grams of Fiber, % of Daily Value	Grams of Fat, % of Daily Value	Grams of Protein, % of Daily Value	Vitamins and Minerals, % of Daily Value

2. Evaluate the information in the table. Which cereal is the most nutritious? Explain your decision.

_____

_____

_____

_____

Copyright © by Holt, Rinehart and Winston. All rights reserved.

Name _____ Class _____ Date _____

Skills Worksheet

Life Skills

Setting Goals
PLANNING HEALTHFUL DAILY MENUS

1. Create a one-day meal plan that meets the recommendations of the Food Guide Pyramid. Record each food in the table below, then indicate the number of servings from each group that it represents.

Meal	Planned Foods	Bread, Cereal, Rice, and Pasta	Fruit	Vegetables	Meat, Poultry, Fish, Dried Beans, Eggs, and Nuts	Milk, Yogurt, and Cheese	Fats, Oils, and Sweets
Breakfast							
Lunch							
Snack(s)							
Dinner							

2. If your body weight is more than that weight which is healthy for you to maintain, what adjustments could you make to serving numbers and sizes? What adjustments could you make if you are under that healthy weight?

_____

_____

_____

3. Do you think you need to change your snacking habits in any way? Explain.

_____

_____

Copyright © by Holt, Rinehart and Winston. All rights reserved.
Lifetime Health   26   Nutrition for Life

Name _____ Class _____ Date _____

Life Skills

Being a Wise Consumer
COMPARING WEIGHT-CONTROL SERVICES

Suppose you wish to lose weight sensibly, but you feel that you need help doing it. If so, you might consider researching weight-control services. Use the newspaper or library resources to select a service. Then answer the following questions.

	Service A:	Service B:	Service C:
1. What dieting guidelines does this service follow?			
2. What part does exercise play in its weight-loss plan?			
3. What type of counseling does this service offer?			
4. How much does this service cost?			
5. Is quick weight loss a priority of this program?			
6. Could this diet be followed in the long term?			

Copyright © by Holt, Rinehart and Winston. All rights reserved.

Life Skills

Making GREAT Decisions
WEIGHT-LOSS METHODS

1. What is the best weight-management plan for children and teens?

_____

_____

_____

2. Give two examples of each of the following ways to manage or reduce your weight.

a. Reduce portion size and high-Calorie food intake:

_____

_____

_____

b. Improve your energy balance:

_____

_____

_____

3. Why is a fad diet not a good choice to include in a weight-management plan?

_____

_____

_____

4. Can diet pills help you lose weight safely? Why or why not?

_____

_____

_____

5. Who should consider gastric bypass as a weight-reduction method? Is this a reasonable method for every obese person to try? Explain.

_____

_____

Copyright © by Holt, Rinehart and Winston. All rights reserved.

Name _____ Class _____ Date _____

Life Skills

Evaluating Media Messages
ADVERTISEMENTS AND A HEALTHY BODY IMAGE

Find two advertisements in a newspaper or magazine—one that might encourage an unhealthy body image for some males, and one that might encourage an unhealthy body image for some females.

1. Describe the first advertisement. What is the primary message of the advertisement? What is its emphasis? How might this advertisement encourage an unhealthy body image in some males?

_____

_____

_____

_____

_____

_____

2. Describe the second advertisement. What is the primary message of the advertisement? What is its emphasis? How might this advertisement encourage an unhealthy body image in some females?

_____

_____

_____

_____

_____

_____

3. Select one of the advertisements and redesign it so that it promotes a healthier body image for all males, or all females. Present your redesigned advertisement to the class, explaining why your advertisement promotes a healthier body image than did the original.

Property of
Raugust Library
6070 College Lane
Jamestown, ND 58405

Copyright © by Holt, Rinehart and Winston. All rights reserved.

Skills Worksheet

Life Skills

Practicing Wellness
AVOIDING ALLERGIC REACTIONS

Suppose you are extremely allergic to peanuts. What are some of the steps you could take in the following situations to help avoid illness?

1. You are at a birthday party and someone hands you a slice of cake. You don't want to offend the person, but you don't know if peanuts are one of the ingredients. What do you do?

   _____

   _____

   _____

   _____

   _____

2. You are invited to cookout for the following week. What might you do before the event to avoid any allergy problems?

   _____

   _____

   _____

   _____

   _____

3. You are with a friend who offers you a taste of his candy bar. You refuse, but he is persistent. What should you do?

   _____

   _____

   _____

   _____

   _____

Copyright © by Holt, Rinehart and Winston. All rights reserved.

Name _____ Class _____ Date _____

Life Skills

Being a Wise Consumer
COMPARING MEDICINE PRICES

Two Drug Bottles

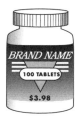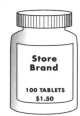

Anyone who has recently purchased over-the-counter (OTC) drugs knows that they can be very expensive. Learning to be a wise consumer by comparing costs before making a purchase can help you save money.

1. Compare and contrast the brand-name packaging with the store-brand packaging. How would you describe the packaging of each drug?

   _____

   _____

2. Which kind of packaging has more appeal? Which do you think is easier to recognize? Explain your answers.

   _____

   _____

3. Why do you think brand-name manufacturers choose the type of packaging that they do?

   _____

   _____

4. Which drug costs less? Why do you think there is a difference in cost?

   _____

   _____

5. What is the difference between generic and brand-name drugs?

   _____

   _____

6. How can you make sure that the contents of two different brands of a drug are the same or are equally safe and effective?

   _____

   _____

Copyright © by Holt, Rinehart and Winston. All rights reserved.

Skills Worksheet

Life Skills

Evaluating Media Messages
COMPARING OVER-THE-COUNTER MEDICINES

Many magazines contain advertisements for over-the-counter (OTC) medicines. Careful review of these ads can help you make good choices about medicines.

1. Skim magazines for OTC medicine ads. For each ad you find, list the magazine source, the product advertised, uses for the product, and the product's active ingredients in the table below.

Magazine	Product	Uses	Active ingredient(s)

2. When choosing an OTC medicine, what are three guidelines one should keep in mind?

_____

_____

_____

3. Select one of the ads. What information does it provide to help you meet the guidelines for safely choosing an OTC medicine?

_____

_____

_____

4. Based on what you know about choosing a safe and effective OTC medicine, would you purchase the medicine described in your selected ad? Why or why not?

_____

_____

_____

Copyright © by Holt, Rinehart and Winston. All rights reserved.

Skills Worksheet)

Life Skills

Communicating Effectively
WRITING A PUBLIC SERVICE ANNOUNCEMENT

Public service announcements (PSAs) can help teens learn about the consequences of drug misuse or abuse. They can also help teens learn to use refusal skills. In this activity, you will plan and design a PSA to educate your classmates about the effects of drugs on the brain.

1. Messages about drug use can focus on either the positive or negative consequences of drug misuse or abuse. A positive-consequence message emphasizes the positive outcome of using drugs safely. A negative-consequence message emphasizes the harmful outcomes of drug misuse or abuse. Messages can also focus on refusal strategies by providing different ways teens can resist peer pressure to use drugs in unsafe ways. Which approach(es) will you use in your PSA?

   _____

2. What message about drug use and its effect on the brain do you want to send to your peers?

   _____

3. Think about the different types of media you can use to deliver your PSA. Which type will you use? For example, you could develop a poster, a written ad, or a radio or television script.

   _____

4. In the space below, write a script, draft a print advertisement, or sketch a design for your PSA.

Copyright © by Holt, Rinehart and Winston. All rights reserved.

Skills Worksheet)

Life Skills

Practicing Wellness
READING ALCOHOL WARNINGS ON LABELS
PART I

Every bottle of alcohol has a government warning on its label.

(1) According to the surgeon general, women should not drink alcoholic beverages during pregnancy because of the risk of birth defects. (2) Consumption of alcoholic beverages impairs your ability to drive a car or operate machinery, and may cause health problems.

1. Why do you think this warning was added to alcoholic beverages?

_____

_____

_____

_____

_____

PART II

Certain medicines can influence the effects of alcohol. The labels on these medicines warn the user not to combine the medicine with alcohol.

2. Read the labels on some over-the-counter medicines in the drug department of a store near you. Find three different medicines with alcohol warnings. List the name of each medicine and the warning(s) in the spaces provided.

a. _____

_____

_____

b. _____

_____

_____

c. _____

_____

_____

Copyright © by Holt, Rinehart and Winston. All rights reserved.

Name _____ Class _____ Date _____

Life Skills

Using Community Resources
LOCATING RESOURCES FOR BREAKING ADDICTION

Find information on alcoholism and lists of treatment centers by checking the HealthLinks Web site or by using library resources.

1. Imagine that your friend or relative is addicted to alcohol and asks for your advice on how to go about breaking the addiction. Contact pertinent resources that are available in your community. List the resources below and identify the types of treatment options each provides.

_____

_____

_____

_____

_____

_____

_____

_____

2. Contact resources that are available in your community for families of alcoholics. List the resources below and identify the services each provides.

_____

_____

_____

_____

_____

_____

_____

_____

Copyright © by Holt, Rinehart and Winston. All rights reserved.

Name _____ Class _____ Date _____

Life Skills

Using Refusal Skills
RESISTING PRESSURE TO DRINK
How would you respond in the following situations?

1. Your friend drove you to a party and then she had four drinks. She says she will never speak to you again if you do not ride home with her.

   _____

   _____

   _____

2. Joaquin drove Roy to an outdoor concert. Roy brought wine. Joaquin, against his better judgment, had about two glasses of it. Now he realizes he cannot safely drive home. Roy insists that Joaquin drive him home. Joaquin's parents are strict, and he will be in serious trouble if he is late or if he calls his parents for a ride and they find out he's been drinking. If Joaquin asked you for advice, what would you say?

   _____

   _____

   _____

3. Assume that you are at a party where everyone else is drinking. When you refuse several drinks, the people at the party start teasing you and will not drop the subject. How would you respond?

   _____

   _____

   _____

4. Rosie is on a date with Tom. They attend a party and Tom has several drinks. Rosie is afraid to let Tom drive her home, but he insists. What should Rosie do?

   _____

   _____

   _____

Copyright © by Holt, Rinehart and Winston. All rights reserved.

Skills Worksheet

Life Skills

Practicing Wellness
ANALYZING CHEMICALS IN CIGARETTES AND SMOKE

There are more than 4,000 chemicals in cigarette smoke. In addition, there are many chemicals in tobacco itself. So far, at least 40 of these chemicals have been identified as carcinogens (cancer-causing agents). Research and write the answers to the following questions.

1. What are some of the chemicals in tobacco or in cigarette smoke that have been identified as carcinogens or dangerous chemicals? List at least five.

_____

_____

_____

_____

2. Many of these chemicals have Material Safety Data Sheets (MSDS), which are required by the federal government and distributed by the manufacturer of the chemical, so that those who handle them will do so safely. These data sheets are available in the chemistry lab of your school. Locate and examine the MSDS for the chemicals you use in chemistry class, or for chemicals in tobacco. After reading these sheets, briefly describe a few safety procedures that users take while handling the chemicals.

_____

_____

_____

_____

3. Is it possible for those who use tobacco or who are exposed to tobacco smoke to take any precautions? Why, or why not? If so, what are the precautions?

_____

_____

_____

Copyright © by Holt, Rinehart and Winston. All rights reserved.

Skills Worksheet

Life Skills

Practicing Wellness
DISCOURAGING FRIENDS FROM TOBACCO USE

Tobacco use causes many problems. There are short- and long-term effects on the user, as well as effects on nonsmokers. People react in many different ways to information about these effects. In each situation listed below, determine what may be convincing to the person and describe what you would say.

1. A cousin of yours is pregnant. She had been a smoker before she was pregnant, but quit while she was trying to conceive. She feels a strong need to resume smoking.

   _____

   _____

   _____

   _____

2. Your younger brother is in middle school and feels pressure from his friends to try smoking. You remember experiencing that pressure when you were in middle school.

   _____

   _____

   _____

   _____

3. One of your friends is considering trying chewing tobacco because he sees many of his favorite baseball players doing it. He figures that he wants to try it just once to see what it is like.

   _____

   _____

   _____

   _____

Copyright © by Holt, Rinehart and Winston. All rights reserved.

Skills Worksheet

Life Skills

Evaluating Media Messages
ANTI-DRUG ABUSE MESSAGES

Use the HealthLinks Web site or library resources to find three news articles that reflect drug abuse in our society. Describe each article below.

1. Article 1

   a. Headline: _____

   b. Topic: _____

   c. What message about drug abuse does this article send?

_____

_____

_____

2. Article 2

   a. Headline: _____

   b. Topic: _____

   c. What message about drug abuse does this article send?

_____

_____

_____

3. Article 3

   a. Headline: _____

   b. Topic: _____

   c. What message about drug abuse does this article send?

_____

_____

_____

Copyright © by Holt, Rinehart and Winston. All rights reserved.

Skills Worksheet

Life Skills

Communicating Effectively
DRUG ABUSE TRENDS

Use the HealthLinks Web site or library resources to research information about how drug abuse trends have changed over time. Find out how abuse of each of the following drugs has changed: cocaine, heroin, LSD, and methamphetamine. Has abuse increased or decreased? Is the drug being used more by a particular age group?

Write the information in the space provided, presenting it in a manner that will discourage teens from abusing the drug. Also indicate the source(s) of the information.

1. cocaine:

_____

_____

Source: _____

2. heroin:

_____

_____

Source: _____

3. LSD:

_____

_____

Source: _____

4. methamphetamine:

_____

_____

Source: _____

Copyright © by Holt, Rinehart and Winston. All rights reserved.

Skills Worksheet)

Life Skills

Using Community Resources
DRUG ADDICTION HELP

The best way to handle drugs is to simply stay away from them. However, if you or someone you care about has a drug problem, you should know where to go for help in your community.

1. Use library resources or local newspapers to research day treatment centers, clinics, and hospitals in your community. List the names of the facilities that you find.

_____

_____

2. Are there any listings for local drug hotlines in your area?

_____

_____

3. There are several self-help groups for drug abusers that are based on the philosophy of Alcoholics Anonymous. Does Narcotics Anonymous or Cocaine Anonymous have a group in your area? Write their numbers below.

_____

_____

4. Contact one of the facilities that offer treatment for drug abuse and ask about the kind of program offered. Ask about the goals of the program, whether special programs for teens are offered, and what the costs are. Write your information on the lines below.

_____

_____

_____

_____

_____

5. Present your findings in the form of a pamphlet or poster that contains this information in an easy-to-read format for fellow students.

Copyright © by Holt, Rinehart and Winston. All rights reserved.

Life Skills

Practicing Wellness
TREATING A DISEASE
PART I

Name the four diseases whose symptoms are described below and identify whether each disease is bacterial or viral.

1. Enrique feels weak and has a fever. He also has a sore throat and swollen lymph nodes.

_____

2. Robin has broken out in a rash all over her body and has small white dots in her mouth. She is tired, too, and has a runny nose, a cough, and a slight fever.

_____

3. Jake has a very sore throat. He is running a fever and has yellow specks on his tonsils. The doctor took a throat swab for a culture.

_____

PART II

Answer the following questions about the people in the situations above.

4. Who should be prescribed an antibiotic and who could not be? Why?

_____

_____

_____

5. For the people who should take an antibiotic, what should they do to help prevent antibiotic resistance?

_____

_____

_____

_____

Copyright © by Holt, Rinehart and Winston. All rights reserved.

Skills Worksheet

Life Skills

Setting Goals
HELPING YOURSELF WHILE SICK

Sooner or later, you may experience the symptoms of an infectious disease. Listed below are some actions that can help make the symptoms less unpleasant. Write down how difficult it would be for you to take these actions, and ideas that might make it easier for you to follow each step.

1. Stay home.

_____

_____

2. Drink plenty of fluids, such as water and juices.

_____

_____

3. Follow all directions that your doctor gives you.

_____

_____

4. Take all the medicine prescribed for you.

_____

_____

5. Throw away used tissues so others won't have contact with them.

_____

_____

6. Wash your hands frequently.

_____

_____

7. Don't share your drinking glasses or eating utensils with others.

_____

_____

Copyright © by Holt, Rinehart and Winston. All rights reserved.

Name _____ Class _____ Date _____

Life Skills

Using Community Resources
PUBLIC HEALTH VACCINATION

What vaccines against infectious diseases are available in your community for free or at low cost? Research your state's, county's, or local public health clinics. Contact one of the clinics for information about the vaccinations and other infectious disease prevention services it offers, and record the information in the list below.

Name and address of clinic:

_____

Phone number or email address of clinic:

_____

Clinic administrator:

_____

Sources of clinic's funding:

_____

Kinds of vaccines that the clinic offers:

_____

Days and times that vaccinations are available:

_____

_____

Other infectious disease prevention services the clinic provides:

_____

_____

Requirements for a person to receive services at this clinic:

_____

_____

Charges, if any, for services:

_____

Availability of information about the clinic's services that can be picked up for free at the clinic:

_____

Copyright © by Holt, Rinehart and Winston. All rights reserved.

Skills Worksheet)

Life Skills

Assessing Your Health
YOUR RISK FACTORS FOR LIFESTYLE DISEASES

You can determine which uncontrollable risk factors for developing a lifestyle disease apply to you.

PART I
Check those uncontrollable risk factors below that could apply to you.

_____ **1.** Males have a greater risk of developing heart disease than females.

_____ **2.** Women have a greater risk of breast cancer than men do.

_____ **3.** African Americans are more likely to develop high blood pressure than individuals of European descent are.

_____ **4.** Mexican Americans have a higher risk of developing diabetes than individuals of European descent do.

_____ **5.** Americans of European descent historically have had higher incidence of heart disease than Americans of Asian descent.

_____ **6.** Americans of European descent historically have had higher incidence of certain cancers than Americans of Asian descent.

_____ **7.** A hereditary tendency to develop heart disease.

_____ **8.** A hereditary tendency to develop certain kinds of cancer.

_____ **9.** A hereditary tendency to develop high blood pressure.

_____ **10.** A hereditary tendency to develop diabetes.

PART II

11. List the controllable risk factors that you can change today.

_____

12. What practices can you follow to reduce your risk of developing any lifestyle disease(s) that you could develop later in your life?

_____

_____

_____

Copyright © by Holt, Rinehart and Winston. All rights reserved.

Skills Worksheet)

Life Skills

Practicing Wellness
ACTIVITY ALTERNATIVES

For each of the activities below, give an alternative that would help lower the risk of cardiovascular disease.

1. When Carla and her family go out for dinner, she almost always orders French fries and adds extra salt on them.

_____

_____

_____

_____

2. Jeanne recently attended a party where some of her friends were smoking. She decided to try just one cigarette.

_____

_____

_____

_____

3. Miguel works in an office all day. He has noticed his weight slowly increasing over the last year.

_____

_____

_____

_____

4. Whenever she encounters a stressful situation, Phyllis feels anxious but always keeps her feelings to herself. So to help herself relax, she likes to eat a double cheeseburger and large fries every day after work.

_____

_____

_____

_____

Copyright © by Holt, Rinehart and Winston. All rights reserved.

Name _____ Class _____ Date _____

Communicating Effectively
PREVENTING CANCER

In the space provided, write a public service announcement for television or radio on the topic of what teens can do to help prevent cancer. Make your announcement attention-getting, and include how each of these terms relates to cancer prevention: (1) tobacco, (2) ultraviolet (UV) radiation, (3) saturated fat, (4) regular exercise, and (5) medical checkups.

_____

_____

_____

_____

_____

_____

_____

_____

_____

_____

_____

_____

_____

_____

_____

_____

_____

_____

_____

_____

Copyright © by Holt, Rinehart and Winston. All rights reserved.

Skills Worksheet

Life Skills

Using Community Resources
NATIONAL AND LOCAL DIABETES ORGANIZATIONS

Finding a cure for diabetes is the focus of national and local groups. Some non-profit corporations exist solely to study the causes and treatment of diabetes. Support groups exist to help people and their families live with diabetes.

1. List some national groups that exist to study diabetes and help people who suffer from diabetes. Find out if local chapters are available in your community or nearby towns.

_____

_____

_____

_____

2. Find out if any support groups exist in which people with diabetes meet to discuss mutual issues affecting them.

_____

_____

_____

_____

_____

3. What information do these groups have on what people can do to prevent type 2 diabetes? Give two examples.

_____

_____

_____

_____

_____

_____

_____

Copyright © by Holt, Rinehart and Winston. All rights reserved.

Name _____ Class _____ Date _____

Life Skills

Assessing Your Health
INVESTIGATING FAMILY MEDICAL HISTORY

Because many hereditary diseases are also influenced by lifestyle choices, doctors use family history to help them modify patients' behavior and decrease their chances of becoming ill in the future. Use the chart below to help you research and record information on hereditary diseases and their treatments.

Hereditary Disease(s)	Description	Treatment
high blood pressure		
rheumatoid arthritis		

Copyright © by Holt, Rinehart and Winston. All rights reserved.

Name _____ Class _____ Date _____

Life Skills

Using Community Resources
RESEARCHING AN AUTOIMMUNE DISEASE

Autoimmune diseases cause many chronic illnesses in the United States.

Choose one of the following autoimmune diseases. Then use library resources to answer the questions.

      alopecia areata   rheumatoid arthritis   Meniere's disease

1. What are the symptoms of the disease?

_____

_____

_____

2. What treatments are available for the disease?

_____

_____

_____

3. What is the usual course of the disease?

_____

_____

_____

4. What resources or agencies exist to help people cope with this autoimmune disease?

_____

_____

_____

_____

Copyright © by Holt, Rinehart and Winston. All rights reserved.

Name _____ Class _____ Date _____

Life Skills

Evaluating Media Messages
DISABILITIES IN THE PUBLIC EYE

What messages about the disabled are prevalent in the media? Use library resources and the HealthLinks Web site, as well as your own observations, to answer the following questions about media portrayal of wheelchair users.

1. How are wheelchair users portrayed in the media?

_____

_____

_____

_____

2. In general, how would you describe the images of wheelchair users? Are they realistic? Do they depict positive role models?

_____

_____

_____

_____

3. Are these images stereotypical?

_____

_____

4. Imagine that you're in charge of network programming for a television station. How might your network portray wheelchair users?

_____

_____

_____

_____

_____

_____

Copyright © by Holt, Rinehart and Winston. All rights reserved.

Skills Worksheet

Life Skills

Setting Goals
ADJUSTING TO ADOLESCENCE

Robert is just entering adolescence. He understands that he will experience many changes during the next several years. To try to prepare for these changes, Robert has decided to make a list of goals to help him cope with the changes ahead.

In the spaces provided, describe what these goals might be.

1. Physical changes (growth spurts, appearance of facial hair, facial acne, increased muscle strength):

_____

_____

_____

_____

_____

2. Emotional changes (new feelings arise, increased desire for independence, conflicting emotions, thinking becomes more complex):

_____

_____

_____

_____

3. Social changes (others may react differently to adolescents, expectations from others may change, relationships with friends become more important):

_____

_____

_____

_____

Copyright © by Holt, Rinehart and Winston. All rights reserved.

Name _____ Class _____ Date _____

Life Skills

Coping
CARING FOR AN OLDER PERSON

David's grandmother has suddenly become ill and can no longer care for herself. Think about the decisions David and his family might have to make about getting care for her and their feelings about these decisions.

1. Could the grandmother come to live with David and his family? What considerations must be made before deciding?

   _____

   _____

   _____

2. If nursing care is required for the grandmother, how might that affect the rest of David's family?

   _____

   _____

   _____

3. What considerations must be made if David's grandmother requires constant supervision?

   _____

   _____

   _____

4. How might David feel about the possible restrictions on his freedom or privacy?

   _____

   _____

   _____

5. How might the relationship between David and his grandmother change if she moves in with the family?

   _____

   _____

   _____

Copyright © by Holt, Rinehart and Winston. All rights reserved.

Skills Worksheet

Life Skills

Using Community Resources
PREPARING FOR MARRIAGE

Answer the following questions to find out about local resources for premarital support and counseling.

1. Where in your community could you obtain premarital support and counseling?

_____

_____

_____

2. What kind of support and/or counseling do premarital counselors offer?

_____

_____

_____

3. What kinds of issues will a premarital counselor address?

_____

_____

_____

4. Why is it important to talk to a premarital counselor before getting married?

_____

_____

_____

5. What other kinds of support are there for people considering marriage?

_____

_____

_____

6. When should a couple considering marriage see a premarital counselor?

_____

_____

_____

Copyright © by Holt, Rinehart and Winston. All rights reserved.

Skills Worksheet

Life Skills

Making GREAT Decisions
BECOMING A PARENT

1. Make a two-column list. In one column, list the reasons why a married couple should consider having children. In the other column, list the reasons why a married couple should consider waiting to have children.

Have Children Now	Have Children Later
_____	_____
_____	_____
_____	_____
_____	_____
_____	_____
_____	_____
_____	_____

2. Imagine that you are a married person. Write a paragraph defending your and your spouse's decision to have a child. Describe the parental responsibilities you will take on and how you will accomplish them.

_____

_____

_____

_____

_____

_____

_____

_____

_____

_____

Copyright © by Holt, Rinehart and Winston. All rights reserved.

Skills Worksheet

Life Skills

Coping
FAMILY RELATIONSHIPS

Answer the following questions about effectively dealing with family problems.

1. Sharon asks her parents if she can attend a school dance. Her parents tell her they would like her to come with them to a family function. Sharon becomes upset and angry. Discuss some ways Sharon could cope with the situation.

_____

_____

_____

_____

_____

2. Anthony's grandmother has recently passed away. He was very close to his grandmother and feels sad and angry. How can Anthony's parents help him cope with these feelings?

_____

_____

_____

_____

_____

3. Sydney's parents often scream and yell at each other. She is afraid that one of her parents will become physically violent. What should Sydney do?

_____

_____

_____

_____

_____

Copyright © by Holt, Rinehart and Winston. All rights reserved.

Skills Worksheet)

Life Skills

Practicing Wellness
CARING FOR THE MALE BODY

During and after puberty, it is important that you take special care of your reproductive and other body systems. Read about the self-care practices below. Then complete the lists to help you to incorporate these practices into your daily or weekly schedule. Whenever you participate in vigorous physical activity, you should wear protective gear to prevent jostling of or injury to the penis and testes.

Keep the penis and the testes clean to prevent skin or urinary tract infections. If you are not circumcised, carefully pull back the foreskin when you bathe. Cleaning the area under the foreskin will prevent bacteria from growing and causing infection.

It is important to identify problems before they have a chance to permanently damage your reproductive system. Using information from this chapter or from the HealthLinks Web site, describe the procedure for testicular self-examination on the lines below so that you can have the information for future reference.

_____

_____

_____

_____

Do you know whom to call if you notice any abnormalities in your reproductive organs? Use library resources to look for clinics that can address your questions about any symptoms you may have.

_____

_____

Things to buy:

_____

Personal habits to develop:

_____

Things to discuss with healthcare professionals:

_____

_____

Copyright © by Holt, Rinehart and Winston. All rights reserved.

Skills Worksheet

Life Skills

Practicing Wellness
CARING FOR THE FEMALE BODY

During and after puberty, it is important that you take special care of your reproductive and other body systems. Read about the self-care practices below. Then complete the lists to help you incorporate these practices into your daily or weekly schedule.

During menstruation, you need to use pads or tampons to absorb menstrual discharge. Tampons are tight rolls of fiber that are inserted into the vagina to absorb the menstrual flow. Pads are worn outside the body and absorb menstrual flow. Both pads and tampons should be changed every four to six hours or more frequently if needed. Leaving a tampon in for longer than recommended or using too high an absorbency for your needs can cause an illness called toxic shock syndrome. If you notice a discharge with an odor or unusual color at any time, you should consult your physician or a gynecologist.

During your menstrual period, bathe or shower every day and carefully clean the pubic hair and vulva. This helps keep the area free of blood and tissue that may encourage infections or at least cause an unpleasant smell to develop. To prevent urinary tract infections, always wipe yourself from front to back after using the toilet. This helps prevent bacteria from entering the urethra.

Many women find that exercising helps relieve menstrual cramps. Others find that a warm bath or a nap helps them feel better. Some use nonprescription medications to relieve the pain. You may wish to talk to a doctor if you frequently have severe menstrual cramps.

It is important to identify problems before they have a chance to permanently damage your reproductive system. Describe the procedures for a breast self-examination on the lines below so that you can have the information on hand for future reference.

_____

_____

_____

Do you know whom to call if you notice any abnormalities in your reproductive organs? Use library resources to research local health clinics that can address any questions you may have.

Personal habits to develop:

_____

Things to discuss with healthcare professionals:

_____

Copyright © by Holt, Rinehart and Winston. All rights reserved.

Skills Worksheet

Life Skills

Practicing Wellness
CARE BEFORE PREGNANCY

A baby's health is affected by the health of the mother before and during pregnancy. Being healthy before pregnancy can reduce the chance of problems during the pregnancy itself.

How will each of the lifestyle changes or behaviors listed below improve the health of the mother and the likelihood of a baby being born healthy?

1. Avoid alcohol, drugs (including caffeine and tobacco). Avoid exposure to toxic contaminants and cigarette smoke.

_____

_____

_____

2. Take prenatal vitamins, prescribed by a healthcare provider, before and throughout a pregnancy.

_____

_____

_____

3. Get regular, moderate exercise, if approved by a doctor.

_____

_____

_____

4. Have all medical conditions evaluated by a doctor before pregnancy.

_____

_____

_____

Copyright © by Holt, Rinehart and Winston. All rights reserved.

Skills Worksheet

Life Skills

Being a Wise Consumer
MAGAZINE ADVERTISEMENTS

Think of two advertisements you have seen recently in a magazine or on television that use a sexual theme to sell a product. Describe them, and then answer the questions that follow.

   First Advertisement

   product: _____

   message: _____

   Second Advertisement

   product: _____

   message: _____

1. Is the emphasis on the product being sold or on sexual activity? Explain.

   _____

   _____

   _____

2. What behavior does each advertisement encourage?

   _____

   _____

   _____

3. To whom is each advertisement directed?

   _____

   _____

   _____

4. In your opinion, does the message being sent in either advertisement show
   irresponsible behavior? If so, how? If not, why not?

   _____

   _____

Copyright © by Holt, Rinehart and Winston. All rights reserved.

Skills Worksheet

Life Skills

Making GREAT Decisions
SEXUAL ABSTINENCE

1. List as many reasons as you can to explain why a teenager might choose to remain or become sexually abstinent. Leave some room after each reason.

_____

_____

_____

_____

_____

2. Next to each reason above, write at least one word or phrase that explains how that teen might feel about that reason. Below are some words you can choose from, but you can also write down words you think of yourself.

independent	frustrated	bad	selfless	wise	stupid
good	glad	happy	proud	relieved	worried
scared	pressured	strong	weak	satisfied	lonely
resolved	selfish	committed	mature	intelligent	healthful

3. Which reason for abstaining from sex would make a teenager feel best about himself or herself? Why?

_____

_____

4. Write a paragraph explaining how following through on a decision to abstain from sex during the teen years would help a teenager build self-esteem.

_____

_____

_____

_____

_____

_____

Copyright © by Holt, Rinehart and Winston. All rights reserved.

Name _____ Class _____ Date _____

Life Skills

Communicating Effectively
COPING WITH SEXUAL PRESSURE
PART I

Describe two situations that you have seen on a television show, in a movie, or heard about that made a teen feel external pressure to be sexually active. What was said or done to cause the pressure?

_____

_____

_____

_____

_____

PART II

What three suggestions would you give to the teen to help him or her avoid the external pressure described above?

1. _____

_____

_____

_____

2. _____

_____

_____

3. _____

_____

_____

_____

Copyright © by Holt, Rinehart and Winston. All rights reserved.

Skills Worksheet

Life Skills

Communicating Effectively
CARING COMMUNICATION

Effective communication and a healthy relationship go hand-in-hand. Honest, open communication requires courage, skill, and tact, but practice makes you better at it. The situation presented below calls for some skillful communication. Read the paragraph and then answer the questions.

At 16, Cherie can't wait to get out of her parents' house. Compared to her friends' parents, she feels that her mom and dad are much too strict: they control whom she can and can't see, where she can go, even how much TV she can watch. One day in school she tells her boyfriend, Brian, that she has thought of a way to move out and be on her own—getting pregnant! Brian thinks this is a bad idea.

1. What could Brian say to convince Cherie that getting pregnant would mean less independence and fewer choices for both of them?

_____

_____

_____

_____

2. What responsible alternatives can Brian suggest for dealing with Cherie's parents' restrictions?

_____

_____

_____

3. How can Brian make sure that Cherie knows that he still cares for her even while he is telling her that her plan won't work?

_____

_____

_____

_____

Copyright © by Holt, Rinehart and Winston. All rights reserved.

Skills Worksheet)

Life Skills

Communicating Effectively
PREVENTING THE SPREAD OF STDs

People who decide to become sexually active are taking a risk with their health and the health of their partners. Sexually transmitted diseases can cause a wide range of health problems that can last a lifetime. Remaining abstinent is the best way to prevent STDs.

1. The only way to determine whether a person is carrying an STD is to be tested by a doctor. Does a negative test result guarantee that a person will not transmit an STD in the future? Why or why not?

_____

_____

_____

_____

2. Why is it important that a person who has been sexually active in the past be tested for STDs?

_____

_____

_____

_____

3. To help you make good decisions, what actions regarding abstinence and sexual behavior could you take?

_____

_____

_____

_____

Copyright © by Holt, Rinehart and Winston. All rights reserved.

Skills Worksheet

Life Skills

Making GREAT Decisions
REMAINING ABSTINENT

Shelly and Sue are at a crossroad with their boyfriends. The girls want to remain abstinent but need advice about why this is a good decision.

What information should you give them about STDs that will help convince them to remain abstinent? Answering the following questions will provide you with much of the information that the girls need.

1. What are five ways that teens can protect themselves from STDs?

   _____

   _____

   _____

   _____

   _____

2. Why is a teenager more at risk of being infected with an STD than an adult?

   _____

   _____

   _____

   _____

3. List four STDs and what causes each of them.

   _____

   _____

   _____

4. In general, what is the difference between the treatment of STDs that are caused by bacteria and those that are caused by viruses?

   _____

   _____

   _____

Copyright © by Holt, Rinehart and Winston. All rights reserved.

Name _____ Class _____ Date _____

Life Skills

Using Community Resources
LOCAL HIV TESTING
Answer the following questions to find out about local HIV testing.

1. Where in your community could a person go for an HIV test?

   _____

   _____

2. What type of counseling does this testing center offer before and after the HIV test? Are the tests confidential?

   _____

   _____

3. What test or tests does this center use?

   _____

   _____

4. How much does a test cost?

   _____

   _____

5. How soon would you get the results?

   _____

   _____

6. What are the laws in your state regarding the testing of individuals? Have these laws changed recently? If so, how have they changed?

   _____

   _____

   _____

   _____

   _____

Copyright © by Holt, Rinehart and Winston. All rights reserved.

Skills Worksheet
Life Skills

Communicating Effectively
THE RISK OF HIV AND AIDS

Many people do not understand that HIV/AIDS is a pandemic. Many people also are confused about how HIV is spread and who is at risk for contracting HIV. Write your response to the following comments using facts about HIV and AIDS.

1. "I am not concerned about HIV and AIDS. It occurs only in poor countries in Africa and in homosexual males."

   _____

   _____

   _____

2. "I can't believe Sally is HIV positive. She looks so healthy."

   _____

   _____

   _____

3. "I read in the newspaper that Joe died of pneumonia, but I thought he had AIDS."

   _____

   _____

   _____

4. "How can a newborn baby be HIV positive? Babies don't engage in high-risk behaviors."

   _____

   _____

   _____

5. "I wonder why my dental hygienist wears latex gloves and a face mask when examining all her patients. It looks so uncomfortable."

   _____

   _____

   _____

Copyright © by Holt, Rinehart and Winston. All rights reserved.

Skills Worksheet)

Life Skills

Evaluating Media Messages
MEDIA AND SEX

1. Make a list of songs, television shows, and movies that portray the negative consequences of having sexual relations with multiple partners.

_____

_____

_____

_____

2. Make a list of songs, television shows, and movies that portray no risk or consequences to having sexual relations with multiple partners.

_____

_____

_____

_____

3. What can you conclude from the number of items on each of the above lists?

_____

_____

_____

_____

4. Do you think that listening to song lyrics and watching television and movies that inaccurately portray the consequences of high-risk sexual behavior can make this type of behavior more acceptable to teens?

_____

_____

_____

_____

_____

Copyright © by Holt, Rinehart and Winston. All rights reserved.

Skills Worksheet

Life Skills: Express Lesson

NERVOUS SYSTEM

Communicating Effectively
WRITING A BROCHURE

Congratulations! You've been hired as the Feel More Travel Agency's newest tour guide. The nervous system is your responsibility, and you need to design a brochure for an adventurous tour of the system. Follow the steps below to help you plan your design.

1. What are the highlights of the tour, must-see destinations, and trendy hot spots?

_____

_____

_____

2. What exciting activities take place in your system?

_____

_____

_____

_____

3. What are the imports and exports of your system?

_____

_____

_____

_____

4. Are there any precautions that travelers should take when visiting your system?

_____

_____

_____

5. Be creative. Make your brochure by folding a piece of construction paper into thirds. Write text that emphasizes the highlights of your tour. Illustrate your brochure with drawings, computer graphics, or pictures cut from magazines.

Copyright © by Holt, Rinehart and Winston. All rights reserved.

Skills Worksheet   **VISION AND HEARING**

Life Skills: Express Lesson

Assessing Your Health
HEARING SCREENING

Hearing screening is easy to carry out and can identify people who may have hearing impairment.

Take the short quiz below. If you answer yes to one or more of the questions, you *might* have a hearing loss and should notify your parent, guardian, school nurse, or primary healthcare provider so that your hearing can be professionally tested.

1. If someone calls your name from across the room, do you have trouble hearing him or her?

2. If you are in a crowded or noisy location, do you have trouble following a conversation?

3. Does it seem as though people are mumbling when they talk to you?

4. If you are in a loud setting, does the background noise drown out conversation?

5. Do you have trouble hearing your friends when you talk to them on the phone?

6. Do family members or friends ever comment that you're "going deaf"?

7. Do you have to turn up the volume on your television or stereo to hear the show or music?

8. Do you feel tired or irritable after long conversations, classes, or other situations that require prolonged listening?

9. Do you often have to ask people to repeat what they have said?

10. Do others leave you out of conversations or become annoyed at you because of your hearing?

11. Do you have difficulty hearing the doorbell ring?

Copyright © by Holt, Rinehart and Winston. All rights reserved.

Skills Worksheet   **MALE REPRODUCTIVE SYSTEM**

Life Skills: Express Lesson

Assessing Your Health
MALE REPRODUCTIVE SYSTEM

Use the information presented in the Male Reproductive System Express Lesson in the Student Edition to help you answer the following questions.

1. Many sexually transmitted diseases lead to an infection of the male's urethra. Why do you think this is the case?

_____

_____

_____

_____

2. Considering what you know about the male reproductive system, list three different steps a male can take to ensure that his reproductive system stays healthy.

_____

_____

_____

_____

_____

3. Based on what you know of how sperm are able to move toward an egg, why do you think it is possible for sperm to impregnate a woman if semen has been ejaculated outside of her reproductive tract?

_____

_____

_____

_____

_____

Copyright © by Holt, Rinehart and Winston. All rights reserved.

Life Skills: Express Lesson

Communicating Effectively
FEMALE REPRODUCTIVE SYSTEM

Use the information presented in the Female Reproductive System Express Lesson in the Student Edition to help you answer the following questions.

1. At which point in a female's menstrual cycle is it possible for her to become pregnant? Can she become pregnant outside of this time period?

_____

_____

_____

_____

_____

2. Do you think a female's reproductive system is ready to bear children while the female is still in puberty? Why or why not?

_____

_____

_____

_____

3. Many sexually transmitted diseases lead to female infertility. Considering what you know about the anatomy of the female reproductive system, explain why sexually transmitted diseases can so easily harm a female's reproductive capabilities.

_____

_____

_____

_____

_____

_____

Copyright © by Holt, Rinehart and Winston. All rights reserved.

Skills Worksheet)

Life Skills: Express Lesson

Communicating Effectively

ADVOCATING PHYSICAL ACTIVITY

One of the benefits of regular physical activity is that it helps build and maintain a strong skeletal system. Exercise promotes health in many other ways as well. For example, it can lower the risk for heart disease and high blood pressure, promote the achievement and maintenance of recommended body weight, and increase strength and endurance.

Despite the well-documented benefits of exercise, many teens in the United States do not get the recommended amount of physical activity. That's where you come in! Imagine that you've been commissioned by your governor to spearhead a campaign advocating physical fitness among your peers.

1. An advocate is someone who speaks out in favor of something. Your assignment is to advocate physical activity. Keeping the learning needs of your intended audience in mind, write a slogan for your campaign.

   _____

2. Brainstorm! List as many benefits of regular physical activity as you can. Then, use library resources to discover additional benefits to supplement your list.

   _____

   _____

   _____

   _____

3. Think about your audience. What benefits of exercise would most appeal to them?

   _____

   _____

   _____

   _____

4. Use the information you have gathered to prepare a public service announcement advocating regular physical activity for your peers. You can make an oral presentation, create a poster or pamphlet, or find another way to communicate your message.

Copyright © by Holt, Rinehart and Winston. All rights reserved.

Life Skills: Express Lesson

Practicing Wellness
EXERCISING YOUR MUSCLES

Your muscles can be exercised in two different ways. Exercise that causes strong contractions of the muscle fibers will result in increased muscle size. Aerobic exercise, which causes moderate contractions, increases the flow of oxygen to the tissues, resulting in greater muscular endurance.

Classify the following activities as resulting in greater muscle size "S" or increased endurance "E." Write the letter of your answer in the blank space provided.

_____ **1.** light jogging   _____ **6.** swimming

_____ **2.** sit-ups   _____ **7.** in-line skating

_____ **3.** baseball batting practice   _____ **8.** pull-ups

_____ **4.** riding a bicycle   _____ **9.** playing soccer

_____ **5.** lifting weights   _____**10.** mowing the lawn
                                                         with a push mower

11. When you exercise, you should spend a few minutes stretching your muscles during warm-up first. What do you think is the purpose of stretching?

_____

_____

_____

_____

12. When you finish exercising, you should go through a "cooldown" period during which you keep moving slowly until your breathing rate and heart rate slow and return to normal. What do you think is happening during that cooldown period?

_____

_____

_____

_____

_____

Copyright © by Holt, Rinehart and Winston. All rights reserved.

Skills Worksheet)

CIRCULATORY SYSTEM

Life Skills: Express Lesson

Practicing Wellness
PROTECTING YOUR CIRCULATORY HEALTH

Research has shown that a diet high in saturated fat and cholesterol can cause a buildup of waxy, fatty material called plaque in some people's blood vessels. As the material builds up, the inner diameter of a blood vessel decreases. As a result, the heart has to work much harder to move oxygen-rich blood throughout the body, often resulting in high blood pressure and heart attacks.

1. Use library resources to find out the American Heart Association's recommended total fat, saturated fat, and cholesterol intake for adolescents. Record the values below.

   _____

2. The recommended caloric intake for teens is 30-60 Calories per kilogram of body weight each day, depending on their level of activity. Calculate your Calorie requirements. (Hint: You can convert your weight in pounds to kilograms by dividing it by 2.2.)

   _____

3. List the items in your favorite fast-food meal below. Then, visit the restaurant to request its nutritional information pamphlet or locate nutritional information online. For each food, record the total amount of fat and the amounts of saturated fat and cholesterol. Total the amounts for the meal. How do these amounts compare with the amounts recommended for circulatory health?

   _____

   _____

   _____

4. What could you do that would allow you to enjoy a meal with your friends, while still protecting your circulatory health?

   _____

   _____

   _____

   _____

   _____

Copyright © by Holt, Rinehart and Winston. All rights reserved.

Life Skills: Express Lesson

Practicing Wellness
ASTHMA

Asthma affects the respiratory system in two ways to make breathing more difficult. The muscles surrounding the bronchi and bronchioles contract to narrow the passages and restrict air flow. Also, the lining of the bronchi and bronchioles produces excess mucus, which can form plugs that block the narrow air passages.

Answer the following questions about asthma.

1. You are out with a friend when she suddenly starts wheezing and is obviously having trouble breathing. You know she has asthma and uses an inhaler. After using the inhaler, her breathing becomes easier within a couple of minutes. What effect do you think the medicine had in her lungs?

_____
_____
_____

2. Asthma attacks can often be triggered by allergic reactions to airborne substances such as dust, mold, cigarette smoke, and pollen. What are some things in your everyday environment that could trigger an asthma attack?

_____
_____
_____

3. If you or a family member were to develop asthma, what changes would you make in your home environment to decrease the chance of asthma attacks?

_____
_____
_____
_____
_____
_____
_____

Copyright © by Holt, Rinehart and Winston. All rights reserved.

Skills Worksheet) **DIGESTIVE SYSTEM**

Life Skills: Express Lesson

Setting Goals
MEETING YOUR BODY'S FIBER NEEDS

Dietary fiber—sometimes called "roughage"—is a complex carbohydrate that makes up part of grains, nuts, fruits, and vegetables. Although the body cannot digest fiber, it plays an important role in digestive health. It regulates the rate at which digestion occurs—in the mouth, the stomach, and the small and large intestines—and it helps ensure that food remains in the digestive tract long enough for nutrients to be absorbed. Finally, dietary fiber promotes regular elimination.

1. Use library resources to find out the current American Dietetic Association recommendations for daily dietary fiber intake. Record the amount below. How does this amount compare with the average daily intake in our country?

_____

_____

2. Record what you eat for one day, making sure to record the amount of each food. Using library resources, determine the fiber content of each food.

3. How does your dietary intake compare with the recommended intake of dietary fiber?

_____

_____

_____

4. Set a goal! The ADA recommends gradually increasing fiber intake to meet its recommendations. Use library resources to locate a list of high-fiber foods. Create a plan that helps you achieve the goal of eating foods containing 20–35 grams of fiber each day.

_____

_____

_____

_____

_____

_____

Copyright © by Holt, Rinehart and Winston. All rights reserved.

Skills Worksheet)

Life Skills: Express Lesson

Practicing Wellness
URINARY TRACT INFECTIONS
PART I
Urinary tract infections are diagnosed when bacteria are present in the urine in large numbers.

1. Name three healthy behaviors you can develop to prevent urinary tract infections.

   _____

   _____

   _____

2. You are experiencing pain when you urinate and think you may have a urinary tract infection. When you go to the doctor, she asks you to provide a urine sample. Investigate the proper method for clean-catch collection of urine. What are the most important points to remember when collecting a urine sample?

   _____

   _____

   _____

   _____

PART II

In the space provided, explain the effect of each scenario on the excretory system.

3. Jacob has been traveling in a car most of the day and hasn't been able to drink much water or eat much fruit.

   _____

   _____

4. Muriel ran errands all day long and put off going to the bathroom until her bladder was uncomfortably full.

   _____

   _____

Copyright © by Holt, Rinehart and Winston. All rights reserved.

Name _____ Class _____ Date _____

Life Skills: Express Lesson

Practicing Wellness
THE IMMUNE SYSTEM AND DISEASE

Use what you have learned about the immune system to answer the questions below.

1. What is the function of the immune system?

   _____

   _____

   _____

   _____

2. How do vaccinations work and why are they important?

   _____

   _____

   _____

   _____

3. What might it mean if you have swollen glands?

   _____

   _____

   _____

   _____

4. What are some ways that you can help your immune system protect you against illness and disease?

   _____

   _____

   _____

   _____

   _____

Copyright © by Holt, Rinehart and Winston. All rights reserved.

Skills Worksheet

Life Skills: Express Lesson

Evaluating Media Messages
HORMONE SUPPLEMENTS

Find two advertisements for hormone supplements. Answer the questions about each advertisement in the space provided below.

1. Advertisement #1:

    a. What hormone is this advertisement selling?

_____

    b. What kinds of results or effects does this advertisement describe?

_____

_____

    c. Other than listing the benefits of the hormone supplement, how else does this advertisement try and persuade you to buy it?

_____

_____

_____

2. Advertisement #2:

    a. What hormone is this advertisement selling?

_____

    b. What kinds of results or effects does this advertisement describe?

_____

_____

    c. Other than listing the benefits of the hormone supplement, how else does this advertisement try and persuade you to buy it?

_____

_____

_____

Copyright © by Holt, Rinehart and Winston. All rights reserved.

Skills Worksheet)

ENVIRONMENT AND YOUR HEALTH

Life Skills: Express Lesson

Communicating Effectively

DEVELOPING AN INFORMED OPINION THROUGH RESEARCH

It has been said that opinions are like noses—everybody has one! However, you can make your opinion stand out in the crowd by learning to develop and communicate *informed* opinions. An informed opinion is one that is arrived at after learning about *both* sides of an argument.

Imagine that members of your community have proposed transforming an old, vacant building into a recreation center for children and teens. The community's enthusiasm for the project is dampened by the discovery that the building was constructed before 1978, when paint containing lead was used. Some area residents are concerned about the possibility of lead poisoning. They believe that the building should be demolished and a new building constructed in its place. Others protest that the new construction will be too costly and that the old building should be renovated. Use library resources to research both sides of this issue.

1. Name the resources you used to research your topic (e.g., newspaper or magazine name and date, TV program name and date, and so on).

_____

_____

2. Are these sources reliable? Explain.

_____

_____

_____

3. Write a report of your findings, including statistics and possible solutions. What are the merits of each approach? What are the drawbacks? How do you feel the problem should be handled? Why?

_____

_____

_____

_____

_____

4. Get your message across! Share your findings with the class.

Copyright © by Holt, Rinehart and Winston. All rights reserved.

Skills Worksheet

Life Skills: Express Lesson

Using Community Resources

LEARNING ABOUT YOUR LOCAL HEALTH DEPARTMENT

Your local public health department promotes personal and community health in a number of ways. Research your city or county health department, or pick up information pamphlets from your local public health clinic to learn the answers to the following questions.

1. What is the name of the agency?

   _____

2. What services does the agency offer to those living in your area?

   _____

   _____

   _____

3. Does the agency have a particular focus?

   _____

   _____

4. What actions does the agency take to help prevent disease?

   _____

   _____

   _____

   _____

5. Brainstorm! How could you increase other teens' awareness of local health resources?

   _____

   _____

   _____

   _____

Copyright © by Holt, Rinehart and Winston. All rights reserved.

Name _____ Class _____ Date _____

Life Skills: Express Lesson

Being a Wise Consumer
SELECTING HEALTHCARE PROVIDERS

Because the quality of healthcare varies, it is important to choose your doctor with care. Follow the directions in steps 1 and 2 to practice working with your parents to choose a doctor who best meets your needs.

1. Add to the checklist additional criteria that you want your doctor to meet.

_____ My doctor must be board-certified.

_____ My doctor must be allowed to treat people at my preferred hospital.

_____ My doctor must have a contract with my health insurance plan.

_____ My doctor must have after-school and weekend hours.

_____ _____

_____ _____

_____ _____

2. Research doctors in your community using library resources. Search for doctors in your area who practice pediatrics. List three pediatricians in the table below. Find out about his or her education, licensure, certification, and hospital affiliations. You should also find out their insurance affiliations and the doctors' office hours. Use these resources to fill out the table, making sure to find the answers to the special concerns you listed in Step 1. Highlight the physicians who meet your criteria.

Doctor's name	Board-certified in pediatrics	Affiliations with my local hospital	Participant in my health insurance plan	After-school and weekend hours

Copyright © by Holt, Rinehart and Winston. All rights reserved.

Skills Worksheet

Life Skills: Express Lesson

Being a Wise Consumer
COMPARING HEALTH INSURANCE PLANS
PART I

Choosing the right type of health insurance plan can be tricky. In the table below, record the features of each type of insurance plan.

Health insurance plan	Description	Benefits	Drawbacks
HMO			
PPO			

PART II

Use library resources to find information on an HMO or PPO that offers services in your area. Then answer the following questions.

1. Are the doctors under contract to the plan near where you live? Would you be able to easily access healthcare if you were to enroll in the plan?

   _____

   _____

2. Does the plan require that you choose a primary care provider from a list? What information does the insurance company provide to help you make an informed decision when choosing a doctor?

   _____

   _____

   _____

3. If you go outside the plan for care, how much do you have to pay? Are there exceptions for emergencies?

   _____

   _____

   _____

Copyright © by Holt, Rinehart and Winston. All rights reserved.

Skills Worksheet)   **EVALUATING HEALTHCARE PRODUCTS**

Life Skills: Express Lesson

Evaluating Media Messages
TRUTH IN ADVERTISING

Dietary supplements and herbal remedies are not regulated by the Food and Drug Administration. Therefore, consumers must be media-savvy in order to evaluate the risks and benefits of these products. Study the following advertisement for a dietary supplement. Then answer the questions.

SuperEnhance 2004

Are you tired and run-down? Is excess weight interfering with your ability to have an active, happy life? Does late-night studying make it impossible to keep your eyes open during the day? SuperEnhance 2004 is just what you've been waiting for! This miraculous blend of all-natural ingredients, used for centuries by Chinese and Native American doctors, can now be your key to a trim, energized, and healthy physique! Just 2 capsules of this revolutionary formula, taken 30–60 minutes before each meal, will set you on the road to long-term health, vitality, and beauty.

Susan L. from Phoenix writes, "I can't believe the difference! I lost 6 pounds the first week! Now I use SuperEnhance 2004 to keep me energized and happy—I have a new sparkle in my eye!"

Bob Q. from Indianapolis writes, "SuperEnhance 2004 was a life-saver for me! My spare tire disappeared, my running times improved, and my hair stopped thinning!"

Ingredients
Ephedra Alkaloids
Caffeine
Willow Bark Extract
Chromium picolinate
Cayenne
Ginger

Join the thousands of happy SuperEnhance 2004 customers. Order a 30-day supply of SuperEnhance 2004 now and receive, with your paid purchase, a bonus bottle of 60—a ten-day supply—ABSOLUTELY FREE! Send check or money order to PO Box 2004, Anycity, Illinois. Allow four weeks for processing.

---

1. What claims are made that should lead you to conclude SuperEnhance 2004 is a fraudulent product?

_____

_____

_____

2. Use library resources or the HealthLinks Web site to learn more about the ingredients in SuperEnhance 2004. What potentially dangerous combinations of substances exist? Which ingredients have little or no value?

_____

_____

_____

Copyright © by Holt, Rinehart and Winston. All rights reserved.

Name _____ Class _____ Date _____

Life Skills: Express Lesson

Being a Wise Consumer
EVALUATING HEALTH WEB SITES

The Internet can be a valuable source of health information. However, along with legitimate Web sites, you'll find some that contain fraudulent or dangerous information.

   To learn how to assess the quality of health Web sites, choose a topic from this chapter. Then visit one of the following Web sites to learn more about your topic: go.hrw.com, www.scilinks.org/health, and cnnstudentnews.com.

1. Use the following WWW Site Evaluation Form to evaluate the information you have located:

WWW Site Evaluation Form
The purpose of the site is clear to the reader:
The intended audience is evident:
The content is presented to inform rather than sell or market a product or service:
The content is presented thoroughly and is understandable to the reader:
Additional links are identified:
The content is up-to-date:
The content presented is referenced:
Reliability Score: **11–13 = Highly Reliable, 8–10 = Fairly Reliable, 4–7 = Low Reliability, 1–3 = No Reliability**

2. Calculate the reliability score for the Internet Web site you visited.

_____

3. Draw Conclusions! Is this a Web site that you would recommend to others as a source of reliable information? Why or why not?

_____

_____

_____

Copyright © by Holt, Rinehart and Winston. All rights reserved.

Skills Worksheet

Life Skills: Express Lesson

Being a Wise Consumer
BUYING SUNSCREEN

Tanning, whether at the beach, in your backyard, or in a tanning salon, is popular and sometimes fashionable. But since radiation from the sun has been shown to be a risk for skin cancer, it is important to use sunscreen. Some sunscreens are more effective than others.

Find out the answers to these questions in order to buy the appropriate sunscreen for your needs.

1. Who needs to use sunscreen or sunblock? Is there any reason not to use these products?

   _____

   _____

   _____

   _____

2. Sunscreens are rated with a sun protection factor (SPF). What is the range of SPF ratings?

   _____

   _____

   _____

3. Who should use sunscreens with an SPF rating of 45 or more?

   _____

   _____

   _____

4. What are some other ways you could help reduce the risk of skin cancer?

   _____

   _____

   _____

   _____

Copyright © by Holt, Rinehart and Winston. All rights reserved.

Name _____ Class _____ Date _____

Life Skills: Express Lesson

Evaluating Media Messages
MARKETING TO TEENS

Did you know that teenagers in the United States pour 84 *billion* dollars into the country's economy each year? That means that the average teen in the United States spends about $3,200, much of it on hair and other personal-care products. Marketing is often targeted to teens because of their high disposable income and their willingness to spend—and advertisers are willing to use unrealistic images to encourage teens to buy their products.

Follow the steps below to learn to evaluate media messages and protect yourself from unrealistic advertising.

1. Gather several magazines, including some that are geared toward teens. List their titles below.

_____

_____

_____

2. Look through the magazines. Locate three hair-care or other personal-care items (skin-care products, nail-care products, and so on). For each, fill out the table. In the last column (Evaluation), indicate whether the advertisement presents teens with unrealistic images. Would you purchase the product?

Product Name	Product Purpose	Advertising Claims	Ploys or Gimmicks	Intended Marketing Target	Evaluation
Ex: CleanSkin Cleanser	*Acne treatment*	*Acne will be cured within 7 days.* *New pimples will be prevented with continued use.*	*Shows attractive teens—both male and female—without acne having fun on the beach. Suggests that product will increase popularity and result in FUN.*	*Teen boys and girls*	*Exploitative; would not buy*

Copyright © by Holt, Rinehart and Winston. All rights reserved.

Life Skills: Express Lesson

Communicating Effectively
ADVOCATING DENTAL CARE

Good dental hygiene can prevent costly tooth and gum disease. Good oral care also involves regular visits to the dentist's office.

Use what you've learned about good dental care to respond to the suggestions below.

1. Imagine that you are giving a presentation to a class of first-grade students. Explain to them the proper way to brush their teeth.

_____

_____

_____

_____

_____

_____

_____

2. Next, explain to your audience why brushing their teeth the right way is important.

_____

_____

_____

_____

_____

_____

_____

3. Create a poster with tooth-brushing information that you feel will appeal to and motivate your first-grade audience.

Copyright © by Holt, Rinehart and Winston. All rights reserved.

PROTECTING YOUR HEARING AND VISION

Life Skills: Express Lesson

Communicating Effectively
CREATING A PUBLIC SERVICE ANNOUNCEMENT (PSA)

The World Health Organization (WHO) estimates that more than two-thirds of cases of blindness worldwide could be prevented. Imagine that you have been hired by the WHO to design a public service campaign geared toward educating the public about ways that they can protect their eyesight.

Use library resources to answer the following questions, then create your campaign!

1. List five causes of blindness, and determine whether each one is preventable and treatable.

_____

_____

_____

_____

_____

2. Think about how the WHO's primary goal of identifying those at risk of vision loss and taking measures to prevent that loss could be met. Then, decide whom to direct your campaign toward. Who is your target audience?

_____

_____

3. Investigate! Use different research resources to identify the primary causes of blindness worldwide. What interventions would be needed to protect eyesight in the populations affected?

_____

_____

4. Be an advocate! Use the information you've gathered to create a 30-second PSA directed to your target audience.

_____

_____

_____

_____

Copyright © by Holt, Rinehart and Winston. All rights reserved.

Skills Worksheet)   **RESPONDING TO A MEDICAL EMERGENCY**

Life Skills: Express Lesson

Using Community Resources
FIRST AID CERTIFICATION

You can complete a short course, sometimes in a day or over a weekend, to learn how to administer basic first aid. At the end of the course you earn a first aid certificate. Knowing first aid procedures could help you save a life. And many employers prefer to hire people with first aid certification.

Research first aid certificate programs in your area, then answer the questions or respond to the statements below.

   1. What can you expect to learn in a first aid certification program?

   _____

   _____

   _____

   2. How long are the courses? How much do the courses cost?

   _____

   _____

   3. Give examples of three situations in which you might need to use what you've learned in your everyday life.

   _____

   _____

   _____

   _____

   4. What types of non-medical jobs might require or prefer first aid certification?

   _____

   _____

   _____

   _____

   _____

Copyright © by Holt, Rinehart and Winston. All rights reserved.

Skills Worksheet

Life Skills: Express Lesson

Coping
HANDLING EMERGENCY SITUATIONS

Being the first person at the scene of an emergency can be scary, but knowing the steps to follow can make it less frightening. The "3 Cs"—Check, Call, and Care—can give you guidance and keep you and the victim safe until help arrives.

   Check the situation. Make sure there is nothing at the scene that can harm you. If there is danger, wait for emergency personnel. Check the victim only when you are sure the scene is free of danger. Try to determine the nature of the emergency so that you can give accurate information to the emergency dispatcher. Call for help. If a phone is available, call 911 (or your local emergency number). If there is no phone, but there are people nearby, briefly leave the victim to ask that one of them call for help. If there are no people nearby, run to call for help. It is important that you quickly call for emergency or medical help *before* you begin to care for the victim. Finally, Care for the victim using only those techniques that you are trained to administer.

1. Naveen saw flames coming from David's house. Then he saw David stumble from the house and collapse on the lawn. David wasn't breathing. Using the 3 Cs, describe below the steps Naveen should follow to help his friend.

   Check: _____

   _____

   Call: _____

   _____

   Care: _____

   _____

2. What are the three basic steps in performing rescue breathing on an adult?

   _____

   _____

3. How are the steps different for an infant? Why do you think the steps need to be different for an infant?

   _____

   _____

   _____

   _____

Copyright © by Holt, Rinehart and Winston. All rights reserved.

Skills Worksheet

Life Skills: Express Lesson

Using Community Resources
CPR CERTIFICATION

Write your response to the following questions on the lines provided.

1. What is the purpose of cardiopulmonary resuscitation (CPR)? In what types of emergencies would CPR be necessary? Give specific examples.

_____

_____

_____

_____

2. Many organizations such as the American Red Cross and the American Heart Association offer training for CPR certification. Find out if CPR classes are held in your community by using library resources. Where are the classes offered? What do they cost? How many sessions are there? What type of certificate is issued for those that complete the course?

_____

_____

_____

_____

_____

_____

_____

_____

3. What are some part-time jobs that might require or desire you to be certified in CPR?

_____

_____

_____

_____

Copyright © by Holt, Rinehart and Winston. All rights reserved.

Skills Worksheet
Life Skills: Express Lesson

Communicating Effectively
BABIES AND CHOKING: A PUBLIC SERVICE ANNOUNCEMENT

Babies are curious and most love to put things in their mouths. Usually, if an object travels to the stomach, it can pass out of the baby's body safely. Some objects, however, can become lodged in the trachea, causing the infant to choke.

Answer the questions below to find out more about preventing choking and treating people who are choking.

1. Refer to this Express Lesson and library resources to learn the signs of choking in infants, older children, and adults. How are the signs of choking similar for infants, older children, and adults? How do they differ?

_____

_____

_____

_____

_____

2. How should you treat an infant who is choking?

_____

_____

_____

3. What do you think is the most important message about choking that parents of infants should receive? Why?

_____

_____

_____

_____

4. Create a public service information leaflet designed to teach parents of infants the message identified in Step 3. Use library resources to gather statistics and other information to help convey your message.

Copyright © by Holt, Rinehart and Winston. All rights reserved.

Life Skills: Express Lesson

Using Community Resources

IDENTIFYING PROVIDERS OF EMERGENCY MEDICAL CARE

Because rapid blood loss can result in shock or death, stopping severe bleeding can be a life-saving effort. Once first aid is initiated, however, it is essential to get emergency medical care as quickly as possible.

To prevent losing valuable time in an emergency, prepare the following Emergency Assistance Information in advance. You can use the information on the list to get assistance or treatment for a variety of medical emergencies.

1. What are the telephone numbers of your local emergency facilities?

_____

2. What is the phone number of the nearest poison control center?

_____

3. List the names, locations, and telephone numbers of hospitals in your community that have emergency rooms.

_____

_____

_____

4. Place a check beside each hospital you listed for Step 3 that is a trauma center. Are other facilities equipped to handle bleeding emergencies or other traumatic injuries?

_____

_____

5. Find out if there are facilities that specialize in care for specific emergency conditions. (For example, there are hospitals that specialize in treating children.) List them here.

_____

_____

_____

6. Write this information on a small card to keep in your wallet. You might want to make another card to post near your telephone at home if you do not already have an emergency numbers list or create a poster that can be placed in your classroom.

Copyright © by Holt, Rinehart and Winston. All rights reserved.

Name _____ Class _____ Date _____

HEAT- AND COLD-RELATED EMERGENCIES

Life Skills: Express Lesson

Practicing Wellness

WINTER SURVIVAL SKILLS

As you have learned, exposure to cold can have very bad consequences. Temperatures do not need to be extreme for the body to lose heat and become dangerously cold. The Centers for Disease Control report that in the past two decades, 13,970 Americans have died as a result of cold exposure. One major risk factor for hypothermia is vehicle breakdown.

Use what you know about cold-related injuries to answer the questions below.

1. Imagine that a vehicle you were traveling in broke down, in wintertime, in a remote area. What would you do to keep warm?

_____

_____

_____

2. One of your companions is becoming drowsy. What signs can help you determine whether he is just sleepy, or is showing symptoms of hypothermia?

_____

_____

_____

3. Investigate! Use library resources to investigate cold-weather recommendations for stranded motorists. Record your findings below.

_____

_____

_____

_____

4. Brainstorm! Being prepared for a cold-weather emergency can make the difference between life and death. Plan an Automobile Safety Kit designed to keep you safe in a cold-weather emergency. What items will you include?

_____

_____

_____

Copyright © by Holt, Rinehart and Winston. All rights reserved.

Life Skills: Express Lesson

Practicing Wellness

TREATING INJURIES

There are different kinds of injuries to bone, joints, and muscles. Knowing what kind of injury a person has may mean the difference between recovery and permanent injury. Use what you have learned about the different types of injuries to answer the questions below.

1. Latoya has slipped down a set of steps. She is holding her arm. Her elbow is swollen and looks misshapen. What do you think is wrong and what should you do?

_____

_____

_____

_____

2. Emilio just finished his best 100-meter race ever, but his calf starts hurting and he limps off the track. What is probably wrong and what should he do?

_____

_____

_____

_____

3. For bleeding wounds, fractures, dislocations, and possible spinal injuries, there are often actions you should take even before medical help arrives. What are these actions and why do you think they are important?

_____

_____

_____

_____

_____

_____

_____

Copyright © by Holt, Rinehart and Winston. All rights reserved.

Name _____ Class _____ Date _____

Life Skills: Express Lesson

Coping
TREATING BURNS

Use what you've learned about burns to respond to the following questions.

1. What are the different types of burns and how do you treat each type?

_____

_____

_____

_____

_____

_____

_____

2. Why do you think it is important to get immediate medical attention for more serious burns?

_____

_____

_____

3. Fire extinguishers can be one way to prevent burns by putting out small fires. There are three basic types of fire extinguishers: class A puts out ordinary materials such as wood, paper, or plastics; class B puts out flammable liquids such as gasoline; class C is used on electrical wiring. ABC extinguishers can be used on all types of fires.

Which extinguisher would be best to keep in a kitchen? a basement or storage area? a car?

_____

_____

_____

_____

Copyright © by Holt, Rinehart and Winston. All rights reserved.

Skills Worksheet

Life Skills: Express Lesson

Communicating Effectively
PREVENTING CHILDHOOD POISONING THROUGH EDUCATION

According to the National Safety Council, accidental poisonings accounted for 12,186 deaths in the United States in 1999. Each person has a 1 in 292 chance of accidental poisoning during his or her lifetime. The key to preventing poisoning accidents is education.

Imagine that you have been assigned to create a plan designed to teach kindergartners about the dangers of household poisons.

1. In addition to this Express Lesson, use library resources to familiarize yourself with the subject of household poisons. What household items pose a particular hazard to small children?

_____

_____

_____

2. Contact your local poison control center to find out what public education materials they offer to help teach small children to avoid household poisons.

_____

_____

3. Think about your audience. What might make poisonous substances attractive to small children?

_____

_____

_____

4. Use the materials gathered from the poison control center to design a creative presentation to teach kindergartners to avoid poisonous substances. Use stories, songs, or skits to teach students how they can recognize harmful substances in their homes. Describe your plan below. How can you make sure students share their new knowledge with the adults in their lives?

_____

_____

_____

_____

Copyright © by Holt, Rinehart and Winston. All rights reserved.

Name _____ Class _____ Date _____

Life Skills: Express Lesson

Setting Goals
SAFE DRIVING GOALS

Complete each of the statements below by writing three goals you can set that will help you practice motor vehicle safety.

1. When I drive, I can make sure I'm prepared by:

_____

_____

_____

_____

_____

_____

2. When I drive, I can help make my passengers safe by:

_____

_____

_____

_____

_____

3. When I drive, I can help prevent accidents by:

_____

_____

_____

_____

_____

Copyright © by Holt, Rinehart and Winston. All rights reserved.

Skills Worksheet

Life Skills: Express Lesson

Communicating Effectively
BE A HELMET HEAD

Bicycle-related head injuries account for about 500 deaths per year. About 153,000 emergency room visits and 17,000 hospitalizations could be prevented each year if riders simply wore helmets! Yet many bicyclists remain resistant to wearing helmets.

Follow the steps below to increase your awareness of the importance of bicycle safety.

1. Research indicates that more adult bicycle-riders wear helmets while riding than middle-school and high-school students. What might explain this discrepancy?

_____

_____

_____

_____

_____

2. Brainstorm! How could you convince others to wear bicycle helmets? What information might promote helmet use? What factors might be obstacles?

_____

_____

_____

_____

_____

_____

3. List three other safety tips that bicycle riders should know and explain why each is important.

_____

_____

_____

_____

Copyright © by Holt, Rinehart and Winston. All rights reserved.

Skills Worksheet

Life Skills: Express Lesson

Being a Wise Consumer
SAFETY AT HOME

Survey your home for potential safety hazards by answering the following questions.

1. Are any of the electrical outlets in your home overloaded (have a lot of plugs plugged into the outlet)? What can you do to help prevent an outlet from becoming overloaded?

_____

_____

_____

_____

2. Are there any electrical appliances plugged in near sources of water such as in a bathroom, or near a sink? List three things you can do to lower the risk of electrocution in such places.

_____

_____

_____

3. Where are matches and/or lighters kept in your house? Is there a safer place for them to be kept?

_____

_____

4. How can you determine if steps or stairways inside or outside your home are free of safety hazards?

_____

_____

_____

5. Why is it important to ensure that your house has a working smoke detector on each floor?

_____

_____

_____

Copyright © by Holt, Rinehart and Winston. All rights reserved.

GUN SAFETY AWARENESS

Life Skills: Express Lesson

Making GREAT Decisions
AVOIDING FIREARM ACCIDENTS

According to the National Safety Council, one in about 4,300 people in the United States will be the victim of accidental gun death. All of these accidents are preventable. Most gun accidents happen at home. Learning what to do if you encounter a gun can save your life or the life of a friend.

Think about what you've learned about gun safety and use the GREAT decision-making model to analyze the following situations. Write in the space provided what you think the person should do in each situation.

1. While John is at his friend Jaime's house, Jaime confides that he knows where his father keeps his hunting rifle.

_____

_____

_____

_____

2. While Ashley was jogging along a path in the woods, she spotted a gun among the leaves under a tree. The gun scared her, and she wasn't sure what to do.

_____

_____

_____

_____

3. While doing homework at his friend Paul's house, Jacob was surprised to see a gun when Paul opened a kitchen drawer to get a pencil. When he asked Paul about the gun, Paul just said, "Don't worry. It's never loaded."

_____

_____

_____

_____

Copyright © by Holt, Rinehart and Winston. All rights reserved.

Name _____ Class _____ Date _____

SAFETY IN WEATHER DISASTERS

Life Skills: Express Lesson

Assessing Your Health
INVESTIGATING YOUR COMMUNITY'S DISASTER READINESS

Every community is vulnerable to weather emergencies and other natural disasters. How prepared is your community? Follow the steps below to assess your community's readiness to cope with a weather emergency.

1. Brainstorm! Identify the individuals or organizations most likely to be responsible for your community's emergency response. Who would be responsible for your community's safety?

   _____

   _____

   _____

   _____

   _____

   _____

2. Choose one individual you identified in Step 1. Use library resources to investigate the individual's role in the community. How might the individual promote disaster readiness and response?

   _____

   _____

   _____

   _____

   _____

   _____

   _____

3. Share your findings with the class. Compare the various individuals' roles to find out how people work together in your community to prepare for emergencies.

Copyright © by Holt, Rinehart and Winston. All rights reserved.

Skills Worksheet)   **RECREATIONAL SAFETY**

Life Skills: Express Lesson

Setting Goals
RECREATIONAL SAFETY

PART I

1. Read the list of items below that are associated with safety and water sports. Rewrite each item in either the Do column, or the Don't column.

swim in unknown waters   wear a life jacket
swim under the influence of alcohol   learn drownproofing
swim with a buddy   swim in frigid water
run or horseplay near water   swim during an electrical storm
dive in unfamiliar waters   check for hidden rocks in diving areas

Do	Don't
_____	_____
_____	_____
_____	_____
_____	_____
_____	_____
_____	_____

PART II

2. Read the list of items below that are associated with safety in the wilderness. Rewrite each item in either the Do column, or the Don't column.

leave fires unattended   extinguish a fire with water or dirt
check weather forecast before hiking build your fire under overhanging trees
build your fire in a windy area   carry a first aid kit, extra food, water,
                                         and batteries

Do	Don't
_____	_____
_____	_____
_____	_____
_____	_____

Copyright © by Holt, Rinehart and Winston. All rights reserved.

TEN SKILLS FOR A HEALTHY LIFE

Life Skills: Quick Review

Ten Skills for a Healthy Life
APPLYING THE SKILLS

The ten life skills can be used to improve the six components of health. Under each component, write the skills that could be used to improve it. Some components can be improved by more than one skill. For each skill, give an example of how it could be used.

Ten Life Skills

1. Assessing your Health	**6.** Evaluating Media Messages
2. Communicating Effectively	**7.** Using Community Resources
3. Practicing Wellness	**8.** Making GREAT Decisions
4. Coping	**9.** Using Refusal Skills
5. Being a Wise Consumer	**10.** Setting Goals

Six Components:

physical

_____

_____

emotional

_____

_____

social

_____

_____

mental

_____

_____

spiritual

_____

_____

environmental

_____

_____

Copyright © by Holt, Rinehart and Winston. All rights reserved.

Skills Worksheet

Life Skills: Quick Review

Making GREAT Decisions

Like other skills, decision-making requires practice—and the GREAT decision-making model gives you a framework to follow. First, complete the steps of the model. Then, apply it to the following scenarios.

1.

G _____

R _____

E _____

A _____

T _____

2. You and your best friend Maya are waiting outside the mall for her mother to pick you up. While you wait, Maya says that she tried one of her father's cigarettes. She talks about how cool she looked smoking and says that she has two more. Maya asks if you want to smoke one with her now. Peer pressure makes you want to say yes. What do you do?

_____

_____

_____

_____

_____

3. Latoya is surprised when a college friend of her brother's asks her out on a date. She isn't sure what to expect and isn't sure if she should accept. If you were Latoya's friend, how would you help her make a good decision?

_____

_____

_____

_____

_____

Copyright © by Holt, Rinehart and Winston. All rights reserved.

Skills Worksheet

Life Skills: Quick Review

Using Refusal Skills
REFUSING TO PUT YOURSELF IN DANGER

Read the descriptions of the following situations, and answer the questions using refusal skills.

1. Susie is on a first date with Tom. She barely knows him and finds herself alone with him in an isolated location. Tom is pressuring her to have sex and she doesn't want to. What are three things that she can do? Assume that Tom ignores each refusal, so that the situation is escalating.

_____

_____

_____

_____

_____

_____

_____

2. Joe and Tammie are at a party. Someone starts passing out drugs. Roger, an acquaintance from school, starts pressuring them to inject some type of drug. What should Joe and Tammie say and do?

_____

_____

_____

_____

_____

_____

_____

_____

Copyright © by Holt, Rinehart and Winston. All rights reserved.

Skills Worksheet

TEN TIPS FOR BUILDING SELF-ESTEEM

Life Skills: Quick Review

Setting Goals
LEARNING TO BE POSITIVE

Juan is having a hard time in school, and he seems to be having trouble speaking up and asking questions in class. He's told you that he has nothing of value to offer to the class and that the other students would think that he is stupid.

Use what you've learned about building self-esteem to answer the following questions.

1. What could you tell Juan about the benefits of high self-esteem that might convince him to make it his goal to develop this quality?

_____

_____

_____

_____

2. What are five things that you might suggest Juan try to help him reach his goal?

_____

_____

_____

_____

_____

3. What are three things that you yourself could do to help Juan?

_____

_____

_____

_____

_____

Copyright © by Holt, Rinehart and Winston. All rights reserved.

DATE DUE

DEMCO 38-297